Dementia Caregiver Guide for the Aging

A Caregiver's Guide to Managing Aggressively Violent Dementia

Michael J Capps

About The Author

Michael J. Capps is an esteemed author specializing in health, self-help, parenting, and relationships. Dedicated to empowering individuals, Capps delves into the intricacies of well-being, providing practical advice for a holistic lifestyle. A beacon of inspiration in self-help, his transformative writings explore the human psyche, unlocking potential and cultivating resilience. Capps extends his expertise to parenting, offering valuable insights for navigating this complex journey. Recognizing the significance of relationships, his works provide guidance on communication and building enduring bonds. Through diverse publications, Capps enriches lives, emphasizing interconnectedness for a fulfilling and balanced existence.

Table of Contents

Introduction

Already, caring for a family member suffering from dementia is difficult on its own before considering the violent and aggressive outburst that may be coming shortly. We wish that the particular episode made the caring folks have in their hands the data, the material, and the motivation to plummet this rough terrain with the compassion and care their patients deserve.

The foundations of our research are laid in the first chapters, whereby we look at the general picture of dementia. Staff members will acquire the board knowledge that is necessary to deliver top-quality care. For this, they must learn the approaches that are used in the diagnosis of dementia and its forms, as well as get tips on communication and solving behavioral problems.

Therefore, we provide clues on what activates illegal aggression as well as the main challenges that come with aggression in people with dementia. In addition to that, we examine closely the upbringing factors that lead certain individuals to exhibit extreme aggression. Apart from this, in our conflict management training, we teach you how to use de-escalation and evaluation methods. One of the priorities in such a circumstance is securing a person with dementia. Our global guide places an emphasis on safety and security in a way that would enable one to create a safe home environment as well as develop an emergency plan.

The caregivers may also experience emotional drain because the illness is not just about their loved one; therefore, we also understand how important it is for them to receive emotional support as well. We offer information on caregiver stress management and how to get help when you need to stop to refresh and renew yourself, from self-care and support groups to respite care.

These problems that are linked to dementia and their resolution are, among others, the medical procedures and the legal implications that, along with the basic care, we put at the forefront. We highlight two priceless values: the autonomy and dignity of an individual with dementia, together with creating favorable living conditions by carrying out favorite activities and engaging them in social relationships.

Caregivers are instructed to read a book with real-life case studies and true real-life stories that have examples and could offer such an opportunity in the lives of others who lead their paths. Along with resources to support the caregiver, we try to give them tools that address their immediate need for help and help them succeed in their duties. We do this through online support groups.

This book, therefore, will be the ideal companion to you by equipping you with the piece of information, the abilities, and encouragement to provide care to people struggling with the harrowing effects of dementia of any kind.

<u>Chapter 1: Definition of Dementia.</u>

The term dementia refers to a general state of diminished memory, thinking, or decision-making that interferes with day-to-day functioning rather than a specific medical condition. Dementia primarily affects the elderly; it is not a typical aspect of aging.

<u>1.1: Overview of Dementia</u>

The word "dementia" refers to a group of illnesses that impair thinking, memory, and daily functioning.

The sickness worsens with time. Though not everyone will have it as they age, it primarily affects the elderly.

Age (more prevalent in individuals over 65)

Hypertension, or elevated blood pressure

Elevated blood glucose (diabetes)

Being too heavy or fat

Thus

Overindulging in alcohol consumption

Not engaging in any physical activity

Being alone in social situations

Depression.

Dementia is a sickness that can result from several illnesses that gradually harm the brain and kill nerve cells, impairing cognitive function (i.e., the capacity to think critically) more than would be predicted from the normal aging process. Although there is no impact on awareness, mood, emotional regulation, behavior, and motivation are frequently altered along with, and occasionally even before, the decrease in cognitive function.

The physical, psychological, social, and economic aspects of dementia affect not just the person with the disease but also their family, caretakers, and society at large.

Symptoms and indicators

Sometimes behavioral and emotional changes develop even prior to memory issues. The symptoms worsen with time. Most dementia sufferers will eventually require assistance with everyday tasks from others.

Early warning indicators and manifestations include the following:

Forgetting details or current affairs

Misplacing or losing items

Getting lost while traveling by car or food

Being perplexed, even in locations you know well.

Becoming disoriented in time

Inability to solve issues or make decisions.

Difficulty keeping up with discussions or having trouble uttering words.

Having trouble doing routine chores

Misjudging the visual distances between items.

Typical shifts in attitude and conduct include:

Experiencing fear, sadness, or rage due to memory loss

Changes in personality

Inappropriate actions

Absence from employment or social interactions

Having little concern for the feelings of others.

Every person with dementia experiences dementia differently, based on their pre-illness cognitive performance, underlying medical issues, and other factors.

While certain symptoms may go away or only manifest in the latter stages of dementia, the majority worsen with time. The need for assistance with personal care grows as the illness worsens. Dementia patients may experience a variety of symptoms, including difficulty eating and drinking, an inability to recognize friends or family, trouble moving around, a loss of control over their bladder and bowls, and aggressive behavior that is upsetting to both the patient and those around them.

1.2: Types of Dementia

Two-thirds of dementia cases are caused by Alzheimer's disease, making it the most prevalent type of dementia.

The second most prevalent type of dementia is vascular dementia, which is linked to blood vessel damage in the brain.

Parkinson's disease and dementia associated with Parkinson's disease are included under the general term "lewy body disease."

By abiding by Australian rules for alcohol consumption, dementia related to alcohol use can be prevented.

Here on this page

Alzheimer's disease

Dementia vascular

Lewy body illness

Dementia frontotemporal

dementia brought on by alcohol

Dementia is linked to the human immunodeficiency virus.

dementia with a younger onset

dementia brought on by the disease Huntington's

Disease Creutzfeldt-Jakob

Where to look for assistance

The term "dementia" is used broadly to characterize the symptoms of many different conditions that affect the brain and lead to a progressive loss of functionality in an individual. It is not a single, distinct illness. Memory loss, disorientation, and behavioral and personality changes are all signs of dementia. These symptoms cause problems for the person's social and professional lives.

Although dementia is increasingly prevalent in those

over 65, it is not a typical aspect of aging. Dementia can be caused by a variety of disorders, each with its own unique characteristics. Most of the time, it is unknown why certain people get certain illnesses.

Alzheimer's disease

Approximately two-thirds of instances of dementia are caused by Alzheimer's disease, which is also the most prevalent type. This degenerative disease damages the brain gradually, leading to an increase in cognitive (thinking and memory) issues.

Amyloid plaques and neurofibrillary tangles are the primary causes of the physical damage in the brain that occurs in Alzheimer's disease. Fibrous patches known as plaques are caused by aberrant protein clumps known as beta-amyloid. The tau protein's twisted strands make up the tangles.

The majority of Alzheimer's cases are not brought on by known genetic alterations. This kind of Alzheimer's disease, known as sporadic Alzheimer's disease, primarily affects those over 65. The signs of familial Alzheimer's disease, a rare kind that is inherited, typically start to show between the ages of 40 and 60. An increase in the creation of the protein found in amyloid plaques is the result of genetic alterations in three distinct genes in familial Alzheimer's disease.

Alzheimer's affects nearly all individuals with Down syndrome, and it strikes them earlier in life than it does people without the condition. The protein that causes Alzheimer's disease's amyloid plaques is produced in greater quantities in people with Down syndrome. This is due to an extra copy of chromosome 21, which houses the gene responsible for producing amyloid protein.

Dementia vascular

The general name for dementia brought on by disorders of the brain's blood vessels is vascular dementia. This blood artery disease damages brain tissue by interfering with blood flow to the brain.

Alzheimer's disease and vascular dementia may have similar symptoms. Some people may experience vascular dementia in addition to Alzheimer's disease. There are several varieties of dementia, with vascular dementia being the second most prevalent variety.

Dementia caused by a strategic infarction

Depending on the magnitude and location of the stroke, a single big stroke may occasionally result in strategic infarct dementia. An extensive stroke may cause the abrupt onset of cognitive or behavioral problems. The specific region of the brain affected by the stroke will determine the kind of symptoms.

In certain cases, dementia symptoms might stabilize or even improve over time if no more strokes happen. The symptoms of dementia may worsen if the individual experiences another stroke or if there is another illness affecting the brain's blood vessels.

Multiple brain infarctions

Transient ischemic attacks (TIAs), often known as mini-strokes, are the cause of this kind of vascular dementia. Disease in the brain's major blood vessels is the source of this. Many times, the strokes are "silent," which means the victim is unaware that they are experiencing mini-strokes.

The brain becomes progressively damaged after strokes, impairing one's ability to comprehend and think clearly. Although mood swings and depression are possible, the symptoms vary depending on where the strokes occur.

The symptoms of multi-infarct dementia may deteriorate with a new stroke, then stabilize for a while before continuing in a stepwise manner.

Dementia vascular subcortical

This kind of vascular dementia, sometimes referred to as Binswanger's disease, is brought on by illness in the tiny blood vessels located deep within the brain, which harm the subcortical (deep) regions of the brain.

Untreated high blood pressure or diabetes that progresses to vascular disease may be linked to subcortical vascular dementia. It is brought on by excessive blood pressure, artery thickness, and insufficient blood flow.

Deterioration of reasoning and cognitive abilities, minor memory issues, difficulties walking and moving, behavioral abnormalities, and loss of bladder control are common symptoms.

Although a person's abilities may vary, subcortical vascular dementia often progresses over time as more vascular damage occurs, resulting in worsening symptoms.

Lewy body illness

The term Lewy body disease (LBD) refers to a group of disorders marked by the development of so-called Lewy bodies, which are aggregates of brain tissue. Clumps consisting of alpha-synuclein protein accumulate within brain cells. These clumps affect particular brain regions and alter behavior, thought processes, and movement.

Consideration and attention span may fluctuate significantly in people with LBD. In a short amount of time, they can shift from nearly normal performance to extreme bewilderment. Hallucinations of the visual kind are also frequent.

The reason LBD is referred to as a spectrum disease is that it has three overlapping diseases, which are as follows:

Lewy body dementia

Parkinson's illness

dementia related to Parkinson's disease

Lewy body development is a feature of all these disorders; however, the diagnosis depends on when the symptoms appear.

LBD can occasionally coexist with vascular dementia and Alzheimer's disease. The diagnosis of LBD can be challenging due to overlapping symptoms, unlike Parkinson's disease, which has well-established diagnostic techniques. Accordingly, the diagnosis is easier to make if Parkinson's disease symptoms

(Parkinson's) manifest first rather than dementia symptoms.

Lewy bodies and dementia

Dementia with Lewy bodies will be the diagnosis if cognitive and behavioral abnormalities are the initial signs.

Parkinson's illness

Parkinson's disease will be diagnosed if mobility problems are the initial symptoms to manifest. Tremors, joint and limb stiffness, trouble speaking, and trouble starting movements are some of these symptoms.

Dementia related to Parkinson's disease

The majority of Parkinson's disease patients will experience dementia-like symptoms. Parkinson's disease dementia will be diagnosed if movement-related symptoms start out and are followed by cognitive and behavioral symptoms.

Dementia frontotemporal

A class of dementias known as frontotemporal dementias (FTD) is characterized by degeneration in either or both of the brain's frontal or temporal lobes. Pick's disease or frontotemporal lobar degeneration are other names for it.

The brain's frontal and temporal lobes are important in mood, planning, self-control, judgment, social behavior, and attention. A reduction in intellectual capacity as well as alterations in personality, mood, and behavior can result from damage to certain brain regions. Damage can also make it difficult to recognize objects or to comprehend or speak words.

In contrast to Alzheimer's disease, memory loss may not occur, particularly in the early stages. The specific area of the brain that is injured will determine the symptoms. Language abilities are impacted by impairments to the temporal lobes, while personality and behavior are the key areas affected when the frontal lobes are initially damaged.

Compared to Alzheimer's disease, frontotemporal dementia (FTD) usually strikes individuals before the age of 70, while it can sometimes affect those as young as 50.

FTD with behavioral variance.

The person's behavior, habits, personality, or emotional responses alter in the frontal or behavioral variety of FTD. Individual differences exist in the symptoms associated with different parts of the frontal lobes that are injured. Certain individuals with behavioral-variant FTD develop extreme apathy, while others experience a loss of inhibition.

Dementia with semantics

The first sign of FTD in the temporal lobe variant is typically a reduction in linguistic ability. Semantic dementia is characterized by a progressive loss of word meaning. Usually impacted are reading, spelling, comprehension, and expression.

Progressive aphasia without fluency

The least prevalent type of FTD is progressive non-fluent aphasia (PNFA), which typically manifests later in life. Fluency in speech progressively disappears. Due to their propensity to create erroneous words, sluggish and difficult word formation, and speech distortion, people with PNFA have trouble communicating.

Inherited FTD

Specific genetic alterations give rise to inherited forms of frontotemporal dementia (FTD). Of all FTD instances, only 10 to 15 percent are familial ones. Roughly half of the cases of familial FTD are caused by two genes: progranulin protein and tau protein. FTD is brought on by a few more uncommon genetic abnormalities. There is genetic testing available for impacted households.

Parkinsonism-17 and frontotemporal dementia (FTDP-17)

There is a type of familial FTD called frontotemporal dementia with Parkinsonism-17 (FTDP-17), which is brought on by genetic alterations in the tau protein gene, which is found on chromosome 17. There are no known additional risk factors for this illness.

Relatively speaking, FTDP-17 makes up only 3% of all dementia cases. Over time, symptoms worsen gradually and typically start between the ages of 40 and 60. Both cognitive and behavioral abilities are impacted by the illness, including rigidity, loss of facial expression, and balance issues (similar to Parkinson's disease).

Finding out that you or a family member has a genetic condition or is at risk of developing one can be upsetting. Through genetic counseling, a person with a genetic disorder and their family can learn more about the disorder and how it may affect their lives. This can help an individual with FTDP-17 manage their disease and the challenges it brings to their health and well-being, as well as the health and wellness of their family, by helping them make educated medical and personal decisions. Parents can also receive prenatal genetic counseling to assist them in making decisions regarding a pregnancy that may be at risk for FTDP-17.

Dementia brought on by alcohol
Alcohol abuse can cause irreversible brain damage, especially if it is combined with a diet low in thiamine (vitamin B1). Because alcohol consumption can lead to

impairments in a wide range of brain activities, many doctors prefer the words "alcohol-related brain injury" or "alcohol-related brain impairment" over "alcohol-related dementia."

The areas of the brain responsible for memory, planning, organizing, and making decisions, as well as social skills and balance, are the most susceptible.

Dementia of this kind is avoidable. In order to lower the risk of alcohol-related health issues, the National Health and Medical Research Council of Australia advises both men and women to limit their daily alcohol consumption to no more than two standard drinks.

Although thiamine deficiency causes Wernicke-Korsakoff syndrome instead of alcohol misuse directly, the condition is commonly referred to as alcoholic dementia or alcohol-related dementia.

The encephalopathy of Wernicke

Alcohol alters vitamin absorption and harms the stomach lining. Wernicke's encephalopathy may result from the ensuing thiamine deficiency.

This condition's symptoms include:

jerky eye movements, double vision, or paralysis of the muscles that move the eyes

diminished muscular tone, unsteadiness, imbalance, or incapacity to walk

uncertainty.

Treatment for the illness can involve high doses of thiamine, which should reverse the majority of symptoms. Death and irreversible brain damage could result from non-treatment.

Korsakoff's illness

Korsakoff's syndrome can develop from Wernicke's encephalopathy if it is left untreated or not treated promptly enough. Additionally, Korsakoff's syndrome may manifest on its own. The brain region crucial for short-term memory is most affected, and it often develops gradually.

Korsakoff's syndrome symptoms include:

Brief (and occasionally extended)
loss of memory
Incapacity to learn or create new memories

Personality shifts
Constructing tales to fill up memory gaps (confabulation)

perceiving or hearing unreal sounds or images (hallucinations)

lack of knowledge about the illness.
If the patient takes vitamin supplements, follows a

healthy diet, and entirely abstains from alcohol, the progression of Korsakoff's syndrome can be prevented. Supplementing with thiamine may help stop additional brain damage from happening.

Dementia is linked to the human immunodeficiency virus.

A consequence of HIV and acquired immune deficiency syndrome (AIDS) that affects certain individuals is human immunodeficiency virus (HIV)-associated dementia (HAD). AIDS dementia complex (ADC), or AIDS-related dementia, was the term used to describe this illness.

Severe cognitive, motor, and behavioral issues that negatively impact daily functioning, diminish independence, and lower quality of life are linked to HAD. While it is rare in the early stages of HIV/AIDS patients, it can become more common as the illness progresses.

Not every HIV/AIDS patient will experience HAD. Roughly 7% of HIV/AIDS patients who are not on anti-HIV treatment are thought to be affected.

The most serious type of HIV-associated neurocognitive impairment is called HAD. Gentler variations have an impact on cognitive abilities (thinking skills like memory, language, attention, and planning), but not to the point where a dementia diagnosis is necessary.

Fortunately, HAD is rare in Australia, where combination antiretroviral medication is the primary treatment for HIV-positive individuals. Still, many HIV-positive individuals are affected by the milder types of HAD, even with excellent treatment.

Dementia with a younger onset

Any type of dementia identified in an individual under 65 years of age is commonly referred to as younger-onset dementia. Another name for it is early-onset dementia.

Although it is far less common in younger individuals than in those over 65, dementia can occasionally be diagnosed in those between the ages of 30 and 60. The prevalence of dementia with younger onset is unknown, and diagnosis can be challenging. Certain types of dementia, such as frontotemporal dementia and familial Alzheimer's disease, are more common in younger adults.

dementia brought on by the disease Huntington's
A hereditary degenerative brain disease that affects both the body and the mind is called Huntington's disease. It is characterized by irregular, involuntary movement of the limbs or facial muscles and typically manifests

between the ages of 30 and 50. A shift in personality, memory issues, slurred speech, poor judgment, and mental health issues are some other indications.

The condition cannot be stopped from progressing; however, medication helps manage psychological symptoms and mobility abnormalities. Most individuals with Huntington's disease have dementia.

Disease Creutzfeldt-Jakob

Prion is the name of a protein fragment that is the culprit behind the transmissible, more highly lethal, and very rare brain disease referred to as Creutzfeldt-Jakob disease (CJD). This condition affects only one person in a million. There are two varieties of CJD:There are two varieties of CJD:

Classic CJD consists of both autosomal dominant types

and very uncommon genetic modes that are inherited from sporadic families.

variation CJD: connected with "mad cow" disease positive.

The first symptoms appear in the form of memory problems, unusual behavior, getting easily lost, and depression. Where the disease progresses—which inevitably it does in a very dramatic way—the patient may lose his or her vision, arm and leg weakness may appear, and body movements may become uncontrollable, followed by the final coma.

1.3: The search for factors and reasons for the disease.

In a variety of studies conducted by researchers, more than a few factors were found that may predict types of dementia. Although these traits do not fully define someone, they cannot simply be altered either.

Years old. Ageing causes a significantly high risk, above 40%, of getting Alzheimer's disease and vascular dementia, among other dementias.

Genetics and ancestry. A lot of genes that give people a people a higher predisposition to Alzheimer's have been discovered by scientists. The fact that not everybody with relatives having this condition gets it, and vice versa, does not mean that those who have a history of the disease are in a higher-risk group for getting it; however, it is generally thought so, since this is the theory that has been common for many years.

Often, it is hard to predict with precision how a person is expected to express the disorder only because of their family history. Individuals with gene mutations are not the only ones affected by these abnormalities. Even nevertheless, they might be common among people without the said gene mutations. Families affected by

Creutzfeldt-Jakob disease, Gerstmann-Sträussler-Scheinker syndrome, or fatal familial insomnia could have inherited the mutations of the prion protein gene. These mutations set off such events that doubled the chance of a healthy person developing certain types of dementia.

Genetic mutations known to cause FTDP-17, Huntington's disease, etc., are also examples of risk factors for dementia.

Besides, the fact is that people in middle age who suffer from Down syndrome have the symptoms of neurological and behavioral Alzheimer's disease.

Alcohol consumption and smoking. From the studies done on this issue, the researchers have shown a causal relationship between smoking and dementia and mental ailments. Smokers tend to suffer from cardiovascular system disorders, among which atherosclerosis and other vascular diseases are included. Because of this, they are more likely to be diagnosed with dementia, which is probably the primary cause of the increased risk for them.

Big drinking apparently raises the risk of dementia, which is accordingly confirmed in studies. In contrast, mild drinkers may not as likely degenerate dementia as heavy drinkers and abstainers toward all alcohol, as some other research indicates.

Atherosclerosis. The deposit of weightless fat (plaque), cholesterol, and other materials in the inner lining of an artery called atherosclerosis takes place.

While the arterial blockage caused by cardiovascular disease often sets off a stroke, and even isolated cases without obvious dementia may be affected, atherosclerosis is one of the major risk factors for vascular dementia. Besides, Alzheimer's disease and endothelial dysfunction may have a relationship, according to a number of studies.

Cholesterol. "Bad" cholesterol, such as LDL, is one of the major causes that, beside stroke, people may have vascular dementia. Another piece of evidence for this link is the fact that high cholesterol is also linked to the progression of Alzheimer's disease in some studies.

homocysteine in plasma. This is evidenced by the fact that most studies show that an increase in the level of blood homocysteine, a humus of amino acids, is a significant risk factor for the onset of vascular dementia and Alzheimer's disease.

Diabetes. Diabetes can cause AD and VAD (Alzheimer's and vascular dementia) to develop. Furthermore, they have been proven to increase the chances of stroke and even atherosclerosis; these are the vascular nuts that cause vascular dementia.

Minimal and non-standard deterioration of cognitive capacity. Despite the fact that not all those with mild cognitive impairment (MCI) will be diagnosed with dementia at a later stage, people who have MCI have a significantly higher chance of developing dementia compared with the population with memory problems that are potentially reversible. This overlapping relationship between depression and dementia is nicely portrayed in the following study. For instance, almost 40% of over 65 adults with mild cognitive impairment had dementia three years later.

Chapter 2: The Role of a Caregiver

Here are some suggestions for dementia caregivers on how to handle violent behavior associated with advanced dementia.

At some point, some people with dementia may exhibit or feel agitated or aggressive toward their family members or caregivers. They fit the following definition:

Brutality

Is a group of behaviors in which a person suffering from dementia exhibits anxiety, either verbally or physically.

Hostility

Is a higher state of agitation characterized by behaviors such as verbal abuse, threats, property damage, physical aggression against another person, or exaggerating in response to slights or criticism.

Aggression and agitation can result from:

The course of dementia disease results in a loss of behavioral control.

Pain, fever, sickness, or constipation are examples of physical discomfort.

fatigue brought on by a lack of sleep.

When one's freedom and independence are in danger, one should act defensively.

frustration brought on by a failure to complete everyday activities.

Fear of surroundings or people because the person suffering from dementia is unable to identify them.

adverse drug response.

Advice for Handling Anger and Aggression

It's difficult to deal with aggressive behavior. Determining the source of the aggression and developing practical strategies for handling it are always beneficial.

It's crucial to understand that, depending on how a person with dementia acts, it may be a means of communication. We can stop them from being angry and acting aggressively if we can figure out what he or she is attempting to say.

Here are a few strategies to control this kind of behavior: Recognize or be on the lookout for behaviors or indicators that point to irritation or aggressiveness. Prior to an outburst, engage the dementia patient in suitable activities to divert their attention.

Make sure everything is safe by removing anything potentially harmful from the area, such as knives, scissors, and sharp objects.

Remain composed and avoid starting a fight. If you react too strongly, it can get worse.

Take your time approaching your loved one, give them comfort, and acknowledge that they are distressed.

When providing care for a person with dementia who exhibits signs of agitation or aggression,

Use brief, basic phrases to describe what you're doing, such as "I'm going to help you take off your shirt" or "We're here to assist you."

Consider whether the work you are doing for the person actually needs to be done right now.

Give him or her some room and time, then come back later to make a gentle second attempt.

If the dementia sufferer is subjected to physical abuse,

To avoid hurting yourself physically, give the dementia patient at least an arm's length of space between you.

Unless the person is endangering themselves or others, do not attempt to control or limit their expression of rage.

If assistance is required, call.

Make sure your loved one's basic needs—such as food, drink, and enough sleep—are satisfied.

Make an effort to keep their daily schedule, surroundings, and caregivers consistent.

Make sure the doctor routinely reviews the dementia patient's medical conditions and prescriptions.

2.1: Understanding the Caregiver's Role

Using one of these techniques could assist you in handling the person you're taking care of's rage or hostility. Depending on the circumstances, you will select one.

Make Room

Give them a brief amount of room. They can be resisting because they believe their personal space has been violated and are unsure of the reason for it.

Avoid Arguments

It's rare that arguing with someone who has dementia can be productive. Even if you believe you have a strong argument, this is still true.

Arguing with someone could only make them more irate. You won't "win," and things can get worse.

It's common to experience emotions such as surprise, discouragement, hurt, or even anger when someone who has dementia snaps at you without any apparent cause.

It's critical to comprehend the causes of rage in dementia patients. This will teach you how to react to and handle these kinds of circumstances.

This article examines a few causes of violence and rage

in dementia patients. It also provides caregivers with some coping mechanisms.

Manifestations of Anger in Dementia Patients

When agitated, a person suffering from dementia may:

Speak up
Toss objects
Engage in aggressive actions like shoving, kicking, or hitting.
Scream and shout!
Attempt to harm you bodily
Make derogatory remarks.
There are warning indicators occasionally. The individual may glare, raise their voice, or swing their arm in the air.

In other cases, you might not anticipate it. The

unpredictable nature of this "no-warning" rage can make it difficult to handle.

The middle stages of dementia are most likely to see the emergence of anger and violence. Other problematic tendencies, including hoarding, roaming, and obsessive-compulsive behaviors, could also exist at the same time.

Six Typical Reasons for Aggression
Dementia patients may become irate for a variety of reasons. A few have to do with the illness itself. Others deal with the psychological effects of dementia.

Absence of Recognition
Dementia patients might not be able to identify their loved ones. Aggression, anxiety, and dread may result from this.

For instance, a wife suffering from dementia might attempt to harm her spouse. She might not act in this way out of rage, but rather out of fear for the "strange man" who lives there.

When Memory Loss Resulted from Dementia

Hallucinations, delusions, and paranoia
Reality distortions are another possible symptom of dementia. For instance, a person could possess

Delusions, hallucinations, and paranoia
These symptoms are not present in every case of dementia. But when they do, managing them can be challenging.

These symptoms are more common in those with lewy

body dementia. However, they can appear in any kind of dementia.

Handling Delusions and Paranoia in Alzheimer's Patients

Compared to Alzheimer's patients, those with frontotemporal dementia may exhibit physical aggression considerably earlier. This is due to damage closer to the back of the brain in those who have Alzheimer's disease.

The brain's frontal regions are in charge of

Empathy

Reflexivity 8 Personality Appraisal
Impulsive actions can result from the absence of these abilities.

Inadequate consumption of food

Research indicates that poor eating patterns and weight

loss may be connected to behavioral issues in dementia patients.

Poor diet can impact mood, energy, and cognitive performance in those who do not have dementia. It can exacerbate impulsive violence and unexpected outbursts in dementia patients.

Making sure the person you are caring for is consuming the correct nutrition will help prevent furious outbursts. It will also contribute to maintaining a tranquil dining area.

Inaccuracies

Communication is affected by dementia. It could be difficult for a person suffering from dementia to comprehend what their caregiver is saying or doing.

It's possible that the person you are attempting to help doesn't know why you're doing it. They might think that you're treating them like subordinates. Conflict may result from this.

Overload in Caregivers

It's normal to occasionally have powerful emotions when caring for someone. You might experience impatience, rage, or frustration. The person you are caring for may sense your emotions even if you aren't expressing them. They might occasionally give such emotions back to you.

Dementia patients can react catastrophically. This is an out-of-proportion, abrupt response to what appears to be a typical circumstance. Care typically sets up these reactions. They may give rise to hostility and rage.

It's critical to keep an eye out for caregiver overload and burnout. Both you and your loved one's quality of life will be enhanced by this.

Strategies for Managing

Using one of these techniques could assist you in handling the person you're taking care of's rage or hostility. Depending on the circumstances, you will select one.

Make Room

Give them a brief amount of room. They can be resisting because they believe their personal space has been violated and are unsure of the reason for it.

Avoid Arguments

It's rare that arguing with someone who has dementia can be productive. Even if you believe you have a strong argument, this is still true.

Arguing with someone could only make them more irate. You won't "win," and things can get worse.

Allow Time

If the person gets upset while you're assisting them with a chore, step away from them for a short while. Give them some time, and make sure they are safe enough to go alone.

You might discover that attempting the identical job after 20 minutes yields an entirely different outcome.

Employ a diversion.

A good distraction is music. Consider playing a few of your loved ones's tunes. It might lighten the mood and put the individual in a position where they can accept assistance.

Individual Conversations

Multiple caregivers might cause anxiety or stress for some individuals suffering from dementia. Restricting interactions to one person at a time might be beneficial.

Aggression and anxiousness can be sparked by multiple people.

Switch up your caregivers.

Routines are typically beneficial for people with dementia. They could favor a caregiver who is reliable. However, occasionally, a different face might produce a different outcome.

Try alternating caregivers if you work at a care facility with other staff members.

Determine the root

Seek out the reason. Behavior can be influenced by environmental and physical variables. Anger and violence can be brought on by discomfort, exhaustion, hunger, or excessive stimulation.

Keep an eye out for behavioral trends. For instance, the individual might have an evening rage.

Consider the events leading up to the outburst. Was

something making a noise? A large number of guests? specific things that happened, or did that make the reaction happen? It will be simpler to avoid triggers if you can recognize more of them.

Consult a physician.

Dementia can occasionally incite such intense hostility and rage that it becomes unsafe for the affected individual and everyone around them. It's time to call a doctor if this occurs.

When managing problematic behaviors, medication should never be the first line of defense. But occasionally, it might be required. This can be assessed by a physician.

Chapter 3: Communication Strategies

Since each person with dementia is different, there are differences in the challenges they face while trying to express their thoughts and feelings. Dementia has a wide range of causes, each of which has a unique effect on the brain.

The following are some alterations you may observe in a dementia patient:

Difficulties locating a term; in place of a word they are unable to recall, a comparable word may be provided.

the utilization of nonsensical rhetoric

a failure to comprehend what you are saying or a limited understanding of what you are saying

writing and reading abilities that have deteriorated due to

a loss of the typical social conventions of speech—an increased inclination to interrupt, disregard a speaker, or fail to react when spoken—and difficulty expressing emotions effectively.

Caregivers must be mindful of their demeanor when interacting with a person who has dementia.

The messages we convey are composed of three elements:

Body language, or the message we convey through our posture, gestures, and facial expressions, makes up 55% of communication. Other factors that contribute to communication include our voice pitch and tone, which make up 38%, and the words we use, which make up 7%.

The significance of how family members and caregivers interact with a person who has dementia is shown by these facts. It's easy to pick up on negative body language, including sighs and raised eyebrows. You can demonstrate your care for someone with dementia and communicate effectively with them by using a variety of techniques or approaches.

It's crucial to always uphold people's dignity and self-esteem because people don't always understand what is being said, but they still feel things. Always be accommodating and give yourself plenty of time to hear back. Touch can be a useful tool to maintain attention and express warmth and affection when it's suitable.

When conversing with a person who has dementia, attempt to:

Keep your cool and speak in a soft, serious tone.
Use orienting names or labels, such as "Your son, Jack," whenever possible. Keep sentences brief and straightforward. Concentrate on one idea at a time. Always give yourself enough time for what you have said to be understood.

To be understood, you might need to make certain hand movements and facial expressions. Giving examples or pointing can be helpful. Maintaining eye contact and demonstrating your concern for them can be achieved by touching and gripping their hand. Laughter and a pleasant grin go a long way toward communicating more than words ever could.

When speaking with a person who has dementia, avoid doing the following:

Confront the individual in dispute; doing so will only make matters worse.

Move the person around, tell them what they are incapable of doing, and then be patronizing by pointing out what they are capable of. Even if the words are not understood, a condescending tone of voice (talking down to people) may be detected. Ask lots of straight questions that depend on a sharp memory. Talk about the individuals in front of them as if they are not there.

A variety of substitute methods of communication have been devised, striving to offer the confidence and assistance that are vital to an individual's well-being. Without realizing it, many family members and caregivers will be employing some of these methods out of instinct without knowing their official titles.

According to validation treatment, it is preferable to enter the person's reality rather than attempt to reintegrate them into ours. In this way, you can establish trust and a sense of security in addition to growing empathy for the other person. Thus, anxiety has decreased.

For instance, family members and caregivers who utilize validation would not challenge a person with dementia if they felt that she was waiting for her children, who are all middle-aged now, to come home from school, nor would they expect their relatives to understand their behavior. They wouldn't refute the dementia patient's views.

Rather, through the application of the validating technique, caregivers would recognize and share the emotions underlying the exhibited behavior. The dementia sufferer's dignity and self-worth are preserved in this way.

Engaging in musical activities with an individual suffering from dementia is an additional productive method of communication. Even after losing other abilities, a person can frequently still enjoy well-known songs and melodies. Some music has the power to evoke strong emotions and memories. It's critical to be ready to react when these emotions are released.

It is necessary to ascertain an individual's musical

preferences in order for this strategy to be effective. You can utilize music for pleasure or as a structured method of treatment. Additionally, it can support the management of challenging behaviors. With their training in using music to help those with dementia, music therapists are able to treat a variety of extremely complicated behaviors.

Examining the past is one technique for reviewing the past. Usually, this is a really fulfilling and beneficial pastime. Memorizing and thinking back on the past can still be enjoyable for a person suffering from dementia, even if they are unable to communicate orally. In the event that the person becomes agitated, it might also serve as a diversion.

Examining the past might bring back happy and peaceful memories, but it can also evoke traumatic and depressing ones. If this occurs, it's critical to pay attention to how the person responds. It is preferable to employ a different type of diversion to lessen worry if their distress appears to be overpowering.

Compiling a timeline of the dementia patient's life can aid in memory restoration and give information to those who could come into contact with them. It can also make it easier for caregivers to learn about the patient and their lives when they visit the home or residential care facility. Like a family photo album, a memorybook or This Is Your Life is a visual journal. Memorabilia such as letters, postcards, certificates, and other items may be included.

A huge photo album that has plastic sheets covering each page will hold up to a lot of use. To prevent placing the person suffering from dementia on the spot with inquiries like "Who is that?" each picture must have a name. It is recommended that each page contain no more than two or three items and that the material be restricted to one topic.

3.1: Effective Communication Technique

A person's capacity for communication steadily declines with dementia such as Alzheimer's disease. Being able to communicate with someone who has Alzheimer's involves tolerance, comprehension, and attentive listening. The following techniques can improve communication between you and the dementia patient:.

Depending on the individual and their stage of the condition, communication changes might take many different forms. Issues that you should anticipate seeing as the illness advances include:

Having trouble putting it into words

Frequently using words you know

describing well-known items instead of referring to them by name.

Readily get distracted.

Having trouble logically structuring words

Switching back to one's original tongue

Speaking fewer times

Depending more on motions than words

Early-stage communication

An individual with early-stage Alzheimer's disease is still capable of meaningful conversation and social interaction; in a medical context, this stage of the disease is frequently referred to as mild Alzheimer's. He or she might, however, find it difficult to express themselves, find themselves repeating stories, or become overwhelmed by too many stimuli. Advice for effective dialogue:

When someone is diagnosed with Alzheimer's, it is important to avoid assuming anything about their communication skills. Everybody is affected by the condition in a unique way.

Don't avoid having a talk with the sick person.

Talk to the person directly instead of through a companion or caretaker.

Give the person your full attention while they communicate their needs, wants, and thoughts.

Allow the person enough time to react.
Stay silent until someone asks for assistance.
Find out what the person can still perform on their own and what they might need assistance with.

Talk about your most comfortable communication style.

This could be via phone conversations, emails, or in-person interactions.

Laughing is OK. Humor can occasionally lighten the tone and facilitate conversation.

Remain steadfast; the person values your friendship, support, and honesty.
Interaction in the intermediate phase

Both older and younger women Grinning adoringly at each other, the longest stage of Alzheimer's disease and one that might linger for many years is the intermediate stage, often known as mild Alzheimer's disease. The patient will need more hands-on care as the illness worsens, and they will have more trouble talking. Advice for effective dialogue:

Talk to the person directly in a peaceful area with few outside interruptions.

Talk clearly and slowly.

Keep your eyes open. It depicts your interest in what they have to say.

Allow enough time for the individual to answer so that they can consider what to say.

Reassure them and show patience. It might inspire the individual to elaborate on their ideas.

One question at a time, please.

Pose yes-or-no queries. Saying "Would you like some coffee?" as opposed to "What would you like to drink?" is one example.

Refrain from correcting or condemning. Rather, pay attention and make an effort to understand what they are saying. To be clear, reiterate what was stated.

Steer clear of arguments. Let it be if the person says

something you disagree with.

Give assignments detailed instructions that are easy to follow. Extended requests could be too much to handle.

Provide visual signals. Give an example of a task to promote involvement.

When spoken words don't seem clear, written notes can be useful.

Late-stage communication

The duration of the late stage of Alzheimer's disease, often known as severe Alzheimer's, can range from a few weeks to many years. The Alzheimer's patient may depend more on nonverbal cues like voice patterns or facial expressions as the illness worsens. In this period, 24-hour care is typically necessary. Advice for effective dialogue:

Face-to-face, approach the person and introduce yourself.

Promote nonverbal communication. Request that the person indicate or make a gesture if you are unable to grasp what they are attempting to say.

Use your senses of touch, sight, hearing, smell, and taste to communicate with the other person.

Think about the emotions that go into words or sounds. There are instances when the feelings conveyed are more significant than the words.

Show respect and decency toward the person. Don't belittle or treat the person as if they don't exist.

It's acceptable to be speechless; what matters most is your friendship and presence.

Follow Alzheimer's News and Happenings

3.2: Nonverbal Communication

A person may employ non-verbal communication if they find that having a discussion is too tough. This could end up being a person's primary method of communication as their dementia worsens. These nonverbal communication tips may come in handy.

The act of communicating without using spoken words is known as nonverbal communication. To communicate with the person you are caring for, you can utilize body language, gestures, and facial expressions. As dementia worsens, these can become some of the primary means of communication for the affected individual.

In situations where they have gone back to using the first language they learned and you are unable to comprehend or speak it, nonverbal communication may be extremely crucial.

There can be alternative channels for someone to express their feelings if they believe that having a conversation is too tough. Drawing, painting, music, poetry, drama, and other artistic endeavors might support a person suffering from dementia in finding their own voice.

A person suffering from dementia may not be able to speak at all in its latter stages. Even so, it could still be beneficial to speak with them and, if it seems right, engage in physical contact with them by holding their hand. They could feel comfortable and connected to you even if they don't say anything or interact at all.

Advice on how to communicate nonverbally with someone who has dementia

Make physical contact to show attention and to reassure the other person. If it feels right, you can reassure them even more by holding their hand or placing your arm around them.

It can be intimidating to sit too close to someone or to stand over them when you're trying to converse. Rather, give them room and make an effort to sit or stand at eye level.

Your body language will be read and interpreted by the dementia patient. Even if the things you say do not upset them, sudden movements, your voice tone, or a tense facial expression can.

Even though this may occasionally seem forced, make sure your facial expression and body language are consistent with what you are saying. Smiling, for instance, can be helpful when discussing enjoyable recollections.

Make an effort to identify the messages being conveyed by someone's body language. If they appear disinterested or preoccupied, try to keep them interested.

Prompts with images can be quite beneficial. For instance, a person can indicate what they'd like to eat by pointing to cue cards or a book with photos of different meals.

Apps that display images or videos of various food kinds are another way that technology can assist with this. In addition to improving communication, this can increase hunger.

The person can find self-expression through singing or sketching enjoyable. Use our dementia directory to see what local activity groups are being held in your area.

Chapter 4: Managing Challenging Behaviors

The Reasons Behind Behaviors

According to some experts, every behavior serves as a means of communication. Confounding or "bad" behavior, therefore, may be an attempt, when the disease has robbed the patient of words and logic, to communicate an unfulfilled need. Resistance-type behaviors might be a reaction to feeling pressured in a given circumstance, losing control, or being confused about what is happening. A patient could be experiencing stress, depression, or pain. It is hypothesized that patients' capacity to handle stress decreases as their neurological systems deteriorate.

Investigative Work

When sifting through patients' behavioral cues, caregivers must exercise perseverance and patience. First, simple physical issues like pain, injury, constipation, infection, moist underwear, tight or uncomfortable clothing, or a patient feeling too hot or too cold should be ruled out.

A patient could be able to shed light on an underlying issue. In one such case, a patient expressed excruciating pain in his foot. An examination in the emergency room found a serious bladder infection. The patient said that his foot no longer hurt after receiving therapy. The most important hint had been given by him himself—that he was in pain—and it was up to the medical staff and caregivers to track it out.

In order to determine whether a patient is tired from sleep deprivation or whether there have been alterations to their routine or surroundings—such as the addition of straightforward holiday décor—caregivers should go over the events of the previous day with the patient. The enemy of those suffering from dementia is change.

Triggers

Six typical triggers for agitation have been identified by dementia experts. These include physical stresses, including pain, illnesses, or constipation; changes in routine; weariness; excessive demands; and a sense of loss.

Unusual Conduct

Anger and fury

While worry, restlessness, and agitation are typical in dementia patients, aggressive behavior is much more concerning. These actions may start suddenly or develop as a result of the patient's annoyance. Examining the causes of behaviors to comprehend the emotions that motivate them is the first step toward managing them.

Examine the circumstances right before the unpleasant behavior, after making sure there are no physical discomforts. What set it off? Taking the time to figure this out could help avert similar accidents in the future. When speaking to the patient, use a gentle, comforting voice and offer assurance. For example, "You seem upset.

I understand that you're upset, but I'm here. Let's get a cookie."

Try switching up your surroundings, doing something unexpected or distracting, like dancing, singing along to a song, taking a stroll, or just going to a different room. Engage the sufferer in creative endeavors or solicit assistance with a task. Take a drive in the vehicle. Play some old-time music, Christmas carols, or well-known hymns. Remember that logic is ineffective.

Straying

At some point, about two-thirds of those who have dementia will wander. Get ready. When searching for someone, "going to work," passing the time when they're bored, or finding somewhere to eat, a patient may become lost. Determining the cause of one's wandering may offer guidance on controlling it. A dementia patient's propensity to wander may be lessened or eliminated with the use of the following techniques:

• Engage the person in daily tasks like putting away the trash, drying dishes, and folding towels. This will lessen anxiety, boost sensations of control, and enhance sleep.

• Get people moving by going for a stroll, dancing, or working out together.

• Install locks that need a key or deadbolts to make the house more secure. Doorknobs should have child-safe covers on them facing the outside (never leave a dementia patient unattended in the house).

• Cover the door with a drape or an oversized photo of a bookcase. Additional options to discourage a patient from approaching a door include STOP! or WARNINGS: DO NOT GO IN.

• A patient may see a large black mat in front of or immediately outside a door as an impassable gap.

• Let your neighbors know that you have a tendency to wander, and make sure they have your phone number.

• Request that the patient wear an ID bracelet from the Alzheimer's Association or MedicAlert. Think about a GPS wristband made specifically for this use.

• Keep a current picture on hand in case a patient does stray.

Speculation or anxiety

This is a common stage that many dementia sufferers go through. They might think that someone is attempting to take their money or possessions. For dementia patients, this feels extremely real; rationalization and explanation will not help. This is not a reflection of the patient's thoughts; rather, it is an expression of the illness.

Allow the individual to speak without offering corrections. Use statements like "Let me help you look for the money" to reassure him or her of your identity and your willingness to assist. Then, turn the conversation to a photo album in the room. Put coins and tiny dollars in a wallet or handbag that you can "find" later if money is a constant problem. Refocus attention after assuring the individual who thinks someone is breaking into the house, saying something like, "That must feel scary. I'm right here. I'll make sure nothing bad happens."

Sundown Syndrome

The phrase "sundowning" describes the increasing state of bewilderment and disorientation that occurs in the late afternoon and early evening. Sundown syndrome affects up to 20% of dementia patients. 3 The severity of this behavior typically peaks in the middle stages of Alzheimer's disease and thereafter declines as the disease progresses.

Sundown syndrome patients may exhibit erratic behavior, such as trembling, pacing, shouting, snapping at caretakers, mood changes, and distrust. As night falls, they could have trouble falling asleep, wander more, and express a "want to go home" feeling. It's possible that they are conscious of their own bewilderment, which can exacerbate things.

It seems that Alzheimer's disease interferes with the brain's ability to control sleep and waking cycles. A lack of structured evening activities, a noisy sleeping environment, physical and mental exhaustion, low lighting and more shadows, discomfort from pain, a urinary tract infection, fecal impaction, etc., medications, hunger, and people coming and going are some other potential causes.

A patient may be calmed by interventions that involve encouraging words, such as "You'll be alright. You're in a secure location. Not fighting or correcting; noticing unfulfilled needs like being cold, hungry, wet, or in pain; moving him or her to a quieter area, like the bedroom, where there are fewer people and sounds; keeping him or her occupied with a favorite activity at the time when sundowning usually happens, like asking for help making dinner, working on an art project, or taking a bath—something the person enjoys doing; and remembering bedtime rituals from their early parenting days.

Think about other methods like aromatherapy, having a pet, having soothing white noise (like the sound of the ocean, crickets, or a brook), eating warm milk or food that soothes, singing a hymn or favorite song, reading a children's book or poem, gently brushing your hair, or giving yourself a hand massage. You can even use multiple of these methods at once.

Problems with sleep

Sleep and wakefulness are regulated by circadian rhythms, which are disrupted in many dementia patients. Maintaining consistent sleep and daily routines, restricting daytime naps to 15 to 20 minutes, increasing daytime activity, such as walking or dancing, avoiding caffeine or serving it only in the morning, providing a light bedtime snack to prevent hunger from being a cause of agitation, allowing as much independence as possible in decision-making, including selecting one's most comfortable sleeping spot, taking melatonin into consideration to promote sleep, and keeping a night light on and the room tidy are some suggestions to help normalize sleep habits.

If these remedies are ineffective, consult a physician. The bewilderment and agitation during the night may be caused by medical issues. A doctor can also go over a patient's prescription list and remove any that are superfluous or producing adverse effects.

Taking a bath

Bathing might make some dementia sufferers agitated. A person suffering from dementia can find it unusual to get assistance with a task they have always completed on their own. Being prepared can be very beneficial.

Prioritize treating pain. Give medication to the patient at least 30 to 60 minutes before taking a bath if they are in pain when moving. Keep all the materials you'll need on hand. Assuage anxieties by outlining your plan of action. Be modest, and make sure the water and room are at a suitable temperature.

Give taking a bath a relaxing, spa-like experience. A patient might eventually come to like taking a bath. Use aromatherapy, play your favorite music, serve a snack or beverage, or spritz your go-to aftershave or perfume. Massage the person's shoulder. Look for enjoyable techniques to engage every sense in a patient.

Permit the patient to take care of themselves as much as possible. Giving options helps someone feel in control again after they've lost so much of it. "Would you like to wash your face or would you like me to help?" is a possible sentence to use. to provide options.

The secret to staying serene is sticking to routines, which include taking regular baths. Agitation may arise if someone suffering from dementia is rushed or startled.

Sexual Practices

One essential aspect of our nature is our craving for intimacy. Individuals suffering from dementia nevertheless require affectionate, secure bonds and tender touch. One way to convey that yearning is through sexuality.

While some dementia patients lose interest in sexual activity, others may still want it. Some dementia patients may engage in inappropriate sexual behaviors, such as undressing, fondling, or making inappropriate sexual advances, when their inhibitions wear off.

Remember that incorrect behavior is not personal; rather, it is a symptom of the sickness. It's possible that a person suffering from dementia won't know when to correctly express their need for physical love or how to control their sexual cravings.

Never show fear or embarrass the individual. Take them on a stroll to a quiet place. This is an excellent opportunity to set up time with a pet, introduce a favorite object, offer a special treat, or use other distraction strategies.

Throughout the day, make physical contact with someone else by holding hands, stroking their hair, or giving them a back rub.

Interaction

Communicating with someone who has dementia can be considerably improved by small things. For instance, are his or her hearing aids in their proper position, are their glasses clean, and do they have new batteries? Locate a spot far from radios and TVs that could distract you. Shut a door or the curtains if needed.

Pay attention to the way you communicate. It can be intimidating to stand over someone, so try to sit down so that you are at eye level. Introduce yourself if there's a danger that the patient has forgotten who you are. Make a nice voice and smile at the same time. Instead of speaking louder, speak clearly, gently, and calmly. Logic doesn't work with people, so don't try to reason or debate with them.

Talk in brief sentences, pausing after each so that the other person has time to assimilate what you have said. One basic instruction at a time, provide it. Upon being instructed to "put on your shoes and socks, brush your teeth, comb your hair, and come to the kitchen to eat your breakfast," a patient suffering from dementia may not carry out these tasks. When it's feasible, use hand signals to get someone to sit down, such as patting the chair. Be patient and wait for a response before speaking again.

Dizziness

Unlike dementia, which progresses slowly over time, delirium is marked by an abrupt decrease in mental abilities. Delirium is curable and needs to be treated right away. Antipsychotics may be useful if nonpharmacological therapies don't work. The symptoms of delirium include an abrupt change in cognitive capacity, an inability to concentrate or maintain focus, a distorted perception of the environment, disordered conduct, a variable or fluctuating state of affairs, and an abrupt onset that can occur within a few hours or days.

A new or altered environment, such as being admitted to the hospital; an imbalance in electrolytes; fecal impaction; urine retention; medication interactions or side effects; pain; stress; trauma; or a significant medical condition, such as an organ failure, stroke, or blood clot, are among the factors that might cause delirium.

Similar to agitation, delirium is frequently avoidable or treated with a calm, familiar setting and routines, activities during the day and peaceful surroundings at night, properly functioning glasses and hearing aids, and relaxing activities like massages, music, or reading to the patient.

Vibrant Light

Putting older people suffering from dementia in bright light improves their mood. The circadian rhythm is highly light-sensitive. According to research, residents of nursing homes who were exposed to strong light for nine hours a day showed fewer signs of sadness and dementia. Additionally, it enhanced erratic behavior, mood, thought patterns, sleep patterns, and functioning skills.

In the study, adding melatonin shortened the time it took to fall asleep and lengthened the duration of sleep. When administered alone, though, it caused residents to become more reclusive during the day. Melatonin did not cause resident withdrawal when combined with strong light therapy; instead, it lessened aggressive behavior. Melatonin should only be administered in conjunction with bright light therapy, according to this research.

Rummage bags

Dementia patients frequently experience a sense of loss—of things, memories, and communication skills. Anxiety or agitation may result from this feeling of having lost something. With an activity that is relevant to their emotions, a rummage bag can help busy, divert, and fulfill a patient suffering from dementia. It can also be a boredom reliever.

Use a large handbag, a men's toiletry bag, or any other bag that holds a variety of everyday goods that could be fascinating to handle, look at, or touch. It is simple to fill with everyday household items. Make sure to stay away from anything that can be disassembled, sharp things, and small enough to ingest. Use your imagination. A bag may contain the following: a set of keys, an address book, a wallet, an indestructible mirror, a coin purse, a tiny plush animal, a non-sharp kitchen tool, a sample credit card, pictures, an old cell phone, a sealed flashlight, or a bottle opener.

Distraction Package

Make a bag or box filled with engaging, surprising, and enjoyable activities that you may offer to others when you need to divert their focus. The patient may eventually associate the box with something so nice that they turn their attention to it right away. Products like aromatherapy or perfume, a sound machine that makes sounds like birds singing, rain, waves, and more, picture books, a music box, lotion for massaging hands or feet, a flannel blanket that can be warmed in a dryer and wrapped over feet, or special snacks could be included.

Reorientation

This is a really useful approach for caregivers. Here are a few instances:

The patient: "Get away from me! Don't touch me!"
Reaction: Get out of the way, alter your appearance (by wearing a different shirt or sweater), or try a distraction like passing food. Allow the person who is available to approach the patient.

Patient: Saying the same thing again.
Reaction: Take the patient's hand and speak the words

together. Next, sing a song you both know to them, then change to the song's original lyrics.

"I want to get out of here!" says the patient.
Start talking about those people in your response by asking, "Where would you like to go?" "How do you get there?" "What is it like there? Who will be there?" Gradually shift the topic of conversation to the location or cars that they have had in the past.

The patient: "Where's my suitcase (or pocketbook)? Someone took my suitcase!"
If this is an object that you frequently worry about, have a suitcase or wallet close by that you can "find." Reaction: "Let me help you look for it."

"I want to go to Sacramento," said the patient.
Answer: "Okay. But you need to get dressed and have breakfast first."

4.1: __Understanding Aggression in Dementia__

Can aggressive behavior be brought on by dementia?

When dementia worsens, a person may occasionally act aggressively, either physically or verbally.

Both the individual and others around them may find this to be quite upsetting. Reducing or simplifying this behavior can be achieved by examining its sources and taking the person's needs into consideration.

Aggressive actions could include:

vocal, such as yelling, shouting, swearing, or threatening physical acts such as biting, slapping, clawing, pulling hair, or hitting objects.

Aggressive behavior is thought by some to be a sign of dementia. While it may be the case, it is more likely that there isn't. It's critical to look past the behavior and consider other causes. Among the possible causes of the person's behavior are:

dementia-related issues, such as memory loss, language barriers, or issues with orientation

their physical and mental well-being; for instance, they might experience pain or anguish that they are unable to express.

the quantity and nature of their interactions with an individual or individuals

their actual environment; for instance, if a room is very dark, the individual may experience confusion and discomfort as a result of being unable to determine their location.

feelings of being uncontrollably out of control, annoyance at other people's actions, or a sense of not being heard or understood annoyance and perplexity at not knowing how to go or at not being able to comprehend what is going on in their environment.

The personality and behavior of the individual prior to the onset of dementia may have been associated with aggression. Nevertheless, this kind of behavior can also emerge in those who have never been violent before. A person's habits and personality can be impacted by dementia.

When it comes to helping someone, it might be helpful to know them and how they respond to and handle situations, as well as their preferences, habits, and past. For instance, if the individual has always been agitated or nervous, their dementia may make them even more so. Considering the viewpoint of the individual is crucial; for further information, see "Preventing and reducing the impact of aggressive behavior."

Dementia can cause a variety of behaviors, sometimes

referred to as "behaviors that challenge," among which aggression is one. Both the person engaging in these behaviors and those who are supporting them may find them difficult. Other symptoms include being agitated and restless, moving about, and acting inappropriately with women.

What leads to violent behavior in dementia patients?

Every human has the same fundamental wants. These encompass requirements that are social, psychological, and bodily. To satisfy these demands, we take both conscious and unconscious actions. This may be more challenging for someone who is experiencing dementia symptoms.

For instance, it can be challenging for someone suffering from dementia to comprehend what is going on around them. For them, this may be terrifying and puzzling. They're probably attempting to get their anxiety under control and return to a more serene state of mind. For instance, they can feel frightened and attempt to push away someone who is attempting to assist them in undressing if it is someone they do not know well or who they have forgotten about.

Aggressive actions could include:

Brought on by the individual being upset due to an unmet need.

the person's attempt to satisfy a craving (for instance, taking off clothes because it's too hot outside and becoming irate if ordered to stop).

the person's attempt to let others know about a particular requirement (they might cry out that they need to go to the bathroom, for instance).

Examples of how various requirements might make a person with dementia act aggressively are shown below.

Bodily requirements

Psychological requirements

Social requirements

Aggressive behavior may be the person's reaction to feeling unappreciated or unable to make a contribution. Encourage the person to accomplish as much for themselves as they can and to follow a regular schedule. Encourage them to become as self-sufficient as they can.

Remaining in touch can provide consolation and stimulation. Assist the person in maintaining relationships with others. For instance, assist in setting up phone or video chats or visits. On tablets or smartphones, social media and messaging apps can be helpful as well. Making sure the person is safe online and doesn't divulge sensitive information is crucial, though.

Encourage the individual to pursue hobbies or worthwhile endeavors. They will feel happier, less bored, and more involved and stimulated as a result of this. They might take pleasure in sensory-engaged hobbies like jogging or creating music, for instance.

4.2: De-escalation Techniques

Having a repertoire of de-escalation tactics is crucial for caregivers in the face of violent behaviors. These methods can help defuse heated situations and guarantee the security and welfare of both the dementia patient and the caregiver. The following are some useful de-escalation methods:

Good Communication: Use a soothing, clear, and soothing tone of voice. Give the person enough time to comprehend your words by using straightforward, uncomplicated sentences.

Minimize clutter and noise to create a peaceful

atmosphere. Comfortable furnishings and soft lighting can contribute to the calming ambiance.

Distraction Techniques: If the person finds themselves obsessing over a certain cause of annoyance, shift their focus to something else that is enjoyable.

Non-Threatening Body Language: Keep your shoulders back and your posture open. Steer clear of direct eye contact, as it may come across as aggressive.

Empathy and Understanding: Make an effort to comprehend the feeling that underlies violent behavior. Show them that you understand their situation and that you are there to assist.

Give Them Space: If things get out of hand, it could be a good idea to leave the room and give the person some time to collect themselves.

Seek Professional Assistance: Do not be afraid to contact medical specialists for assistance if aggressive behaviors continue or worsen.

Keep in mind that each person is different, so what suits one may not suit another. It's critical to have patience, flexibility, and an openness to trying out various strategies.

Techniques for Calming

After an angry episode, calming techniques can help a person with dementia relax and avoid future aggressive behaviors. These methods can improve the quality of life for those who are caring for those who have dementia and help create a more tranquil atmosphere. Here are a few useful methods for relaxing:

Keeping a Regular Schedule: People suffering from dementia frequently find solace in routine. Retaining a regular daily schedule helps ease confusion and offers security.

Promoting Frequent Exercise: Engaging in regular physical activity might help to calm down and lessen anxiety. This could be as easy as taking a daily stroll or doing mild workouts that are appropriate for their level of ability.

Establishing a Comfortable Environment: Make sure the setting is recognizable, secure, and cozy. This can be playing their favorite music or keeping their favorite things around.

Mindful Breathing: Taking deep, deliberate breaths with the person can help them relax and feel less agitated.

Taking Part in Fun Activities: It can be soothing to include the person in fun activities. This could be seeing old family photos, engaging in a pastime, or doing easy chores like folding laundry.

Ensuring that the individual has a restful night's sleep can aid in mitigating agitation. This can involve keeping a regular sleep routine and setting up a relaxing and cozy sleeping space.

Nutrition and Hydration: Keeping the individual hydrated and well-nourished can also improve their general health and mood.

Remember, when using these strategies, it's critical to

exercise patience and flexibility. It's acceptable if what works one day doesn't work the next. The intention is to establish a serene and comforting atmosphere that upholds and honors the dignity of the dementia sufferer.

Chapter 5: Promoting a Safe Environment

A dementia patient's ideal living situation is one that promotes their maximum level of independence and happiness. It's critical that a person with dementia become accustomed to their surroundings and habits.

Their living space ought to assist them in determining their current location and their desired destination. Confusion and disorientation may worsen as a result of environmental changes.

Here are some pointers for creating a secure environment in the house for the dementia patient:

Maintain a clutter-free atmosphere by arranging the furnishings in an easy and regular manner.
Eliminate any loose carpets and seal any potentially dangerous carpet edges.
To make it easier for someone to find their way to the restroom at night, install nightlights in the restroom and hallways.
Get rid of all outdated prescription drugs and dangerous items like kerosene, or store them carefully.

Take away any hot water bottles and electric blankets

that can pose a risk to the safety of a person suffering from dementia.

Install safety switches in your home; they are now advised.

Make use of appliances with automated shut-off features, such as hot water jugs.

Column heaters are a safer alternative to more potentially hazardous heating methods like bar radiators.

Verify that items such as toasters and heaters do not pose any risks to safety.

Appliances with long electrical cables should be replaced with retractable or coiled cords.

To regulate the temperature of the water that flows from the hot water taps, think about thermostats.

Verify that smoke alarms are operating properly. Someone with dementia might require assistance from another person to check the alarm's loudness and battery.

Safety for dementia patients outside the home

Certain individuals suffering from dementia may experience disorientation and become lost in unfamiliar or even familiar environments. It is crucial that they always have proper identification, which should include their name, address, and emergency contact information. The perfect accessory is an identity bracelet.

The following are some pointers for creating a secure environment outside the house for the dementia patient:

Maintain well-swept pathways free of overhanging trees.

Verify the gate catches.

Take out any toxic plants and dispose of any dangerous materials in garages and sheds.

5.1: Home Safety Tips

To look for any safety issues, going room by room through the house could be helpful. The following checklist might help you get rid of dangers and create a safer atmosphere in your house.

Getting inside the house

Route

Among the safety checkpoints are:

layout of the home, including the non-slip flooring, windows, doors, and heating. It also includes uncluttered lighting.

Living area security points consist of:

chair heights with furniture projecting.

Cooking

Among the safety checkpoints are:

combustible floor materials, taps, and gas and electrical equipment

Kettle poisoning: storage cabinets

Drainage in floor electrical connections: Verify that they are not in potential contact with sources of heat or water.

Restroom

Among the safety checkpoints are:

floor; how slick; chemicals from hot water thermostat control; storage; toilet paper height; and visible.

Clothes

Among the safety checkpoints are:

Poisons: make sure they are kept out of potential contact with water by checking the storage drainage in floor electrical connections.

Safety checks in bedrooms include:

A bedroom chair at bed height for getting dressed.

Straying

Ensuring the safety of the dementia patient when they

leave the house is just as crucial as making the house safer.

Among the safety checkpoints are:

Identification bracelet; emergency contact number in wallet; door, window, and gate bells.

Helping the person with dementia become more independent

Helps for self-sufficiency and security comprise:

Railings next to the bath, shower, and toilet to offer support and balance; hand-held shower hoses that help users control the water's flow; shower chairs or seats that let users sit while taking a shower instead of lowering themselves into the tub;

Large, easy-to-read calendars and clocks that make it easier to tell the time and date; heat sensors or alarms that sound in the event of an emergency; and a list of contact information in big print near the phone that makes it easier to keep in touch.

Every Australian state and territory has an independent living center that provides a range of services aimed at encouraging safe living. A variety of items, such as temperature regulators for hot water services, smoke detectors, and monitoring services, are available for information. There's also advice about designing and remodeling homes.

Alterations to the surroundings for dementia patients

Problem solving necessitates ongoing planning and review. Any modifications you make to a person with dementia's surroundings should be guided by the following principles:

When feasible, involve the dementia patient in problem-solving and decision-making on alterations to their surroundings.

Verify that the changes are appropriate for that person.

Address particular issues rather than introducing generic changes.

Minimize alteration and preserve the familiar.

Maximize their independence and build on their skills.

Start with easy fixes.

Ensure that the alterations are respectable and reminiscent of home.

Adjustments must be suitable for the person's age and cultural background.

Consider the hazards and strive to strike a balance between freedom and safety.

Ensure that the workplace is safe for employees, caregivers, and family members.

5.2: Using Assistive Devices

Assistive Dementia Technology

An elderly person with dementia can maintain as much independence as possible in their own home with the use of assistive technologies. Thanks to technological advancements, technology that can assist people with the condition with their cognitive problems and physical issues has been developed.

Perhaps you are concerned for the safety of a loved one you are caring for who has dementia. Or perhaps you are the one who has the illness and finds it difficult to manage on your own. We cover everything you need to know about the dementia technology that is available to you in this article. We define assistive dementia technology, discuss its many advantages for daily living, and provide information on how dementia patients can get and use it.

Assistive Technology : What is it?

Dementia technology, often known as assistive technology, is the term used to describe tools and systems that help a person with dementia carry out daily duties. A person with dementia-related memory problems, mobility difficulties, and frailty can benefit from the assistance of these tools and equipment.

In recent years, there has been a remarkable evolution in the use of technology in dementia care. Assistive technology includes everything from smart home automation systems to smart phone apps that help with dementia communication. It also includes alarms that remind you to do activities.

Assistive technology can help a person with dementia make the most of their life in a number of ways. In addition to enhancing safety and independence, assistive technology for dementia patients can also aid in monitoring their health and well-being. In particular, assistive technology can be useful for:

Memory problems

assistance in organizing certain daily tasks, mobility, and movement

Staying safe indoors and outside Communication (spoken and auditory)

Socialization

Increasing independence and self-assurance

There are various varieties of assistive technology for dementia.

The kinds of gadgets and alert systems that can help someone with dementia live well are listed below.

mobile phones

Older folks are using mobile smartphone technology more and more to stay connected to loved ones and manage their lives. They let you utilize 'apps' and email in addition to making and receiving calls and text messages. They can support a person's independence and serve as communication aids for dementia in a number of ways, including:

The majority of mobile cellphones allow you to utilize the calendar or view the time and date.

You can use phone alarms to remind yourself to do tasks at specific times of the day.

It can be used to access additional dementia-related assistive technology, such as multimedia services like TV program scheduling, thermostats for controlling the warmth in the house, and in-home webcams.

They can use the calendar feature to assist your loved one in remembering their doctor's or hospital appointments so they don't forget them. Today, most businesses employ text reminders to let patients know about their appointments via mobile devices.

Mobile cell phones can be used for online shopping, and frequently visited websites can be saved in a "favorites" file.

When a dementia patient needs your help or has an

emergency, they can use these as safety devices to make sure they can always get in touch with someone.

Alarms and clocks

Not everyone will be at ease using the technology on smartphones. There are numerous digital LCD clocks and radio-controlled models available. These are simple to see since they feature huge digits. Certain clocks and gadgets employ light or graphic representation to indicate whether it is morning, afternoon, or nighttime. Those suffering from dementia may find it difficult to distinguish between day and night; therefore, this is quite useful to them.

GPS monitoring tools

The ideal safety equipment for people with dementia who occasionally go lost are tracking devices. The dementia patient wears the tracking device, and if they walk out of a certain area—for example, the house—the alert system will sound an alarm to a family member. They provide much-needed comfort to family members, knowing that their loved one is secure.

Intelligent gadgets

Memory issues in a person with dementia can be helped by smart gadgets such as the Apple HomePod, Google Home, and Amazon Echo. These voice-activated gadgets can be programmed to send out reminders to your loved one to remind them to do specific chores, including taking their medication. You can also inquire about things like the time and date. If your loved one is at ease with technology, they can request that a grocery list be made or that a television show be recorded using more sophisticated functions. Of course, in order to utilize these functions, a Wi-Fi setup in the house is required.

Device for monitoring electrical appliances

Knowing your loved one is safe will be extremely important to you if you do not live with them. A recent technological advancement tracks how electrical appliances are used in the house and notifies you when they are on or off. As a result, you will know if they have left the cooker on for an extended period of time, so you can react accordingly

Cameras within the house

Another excellent option to guarantee your loved one's safety and give you peace of mind is to install cameras in their home. Then, you can connect a variety of gadgets to a smartphone app, enabling you to know your loved one's whereabouts in real time from anywhere.

Electronic drug administration
Digital pill dispensers and boxes are widely available on the market. They send out an alert to let the family caregiver or people suffering from dementia know when it's time to take their prescription. Certain dispensers can be connected to a watch's vibrating alarm. With the use of this technology, people with dementia can safely and successfully control their medicine.

Big picture phones

Many individuals with dementia have trouble remembering phone numbers, which can be problematic when they need to contact someone right away or in an emergency. Large number buttons, commonly called numbers, are pre-programmed into these phones. Certain phones feature transparent buttons with pictures of their loved ones on them, which, when pressed, will call the person in question.

Assistive Technology Selective For Dementia

A few factors need to be taken into account while selecting assistive technology for dementia patients. Consider speaking with an occupational therapist to find out what equipment would be most appropriate for your loved one's needs. They will carry out a thorough evaluation of their demands and desired lifestyle, and they will share their opinions about what would make life simpler with the family.

In order to respect your loved one's decisions and wishes, it is always crucial to make sure they are included in what is being planned for them. It's possible that your loved one needs assistance and support to incorporate new technology into their life since they are uncomfortable with it. No choice that infringes on someone's privacy or freedom should be made.

Certain technology may not be appropriate depending on where your loved one is in their dementia journey, and it will never be able to replace the one-on-one care that your loved one requires from a family member or professional caregiver. It is important to remember that face-to-face communication with loved ones is still the best way to stay in touch during dementia.

This could negatively affect someone's general wellbeing and cause them to feel socially isolated.

When selecting assistive technology for dementia, keep the following factors in mind:

if it is necessary, or if there is another way for you to receive the support.

Which technology would fulfill your demands the best?

Your device preferences and usage style, as well as any potential changes over time and any additional medical conditions that can impact your technology use (e.g., vision or hearing impairments),

the extent of your social support system and whether it will be necessary for you to use the technology.

how seamlessly the technology will integrate into your daily routine.

whether a phone line or internet connection are needed for the technology

The price of the technology

The price of dementia-related assistive technology

For some dementia patients, the cost of safety equipment and dementia technology can be high. The technology required to enable people to maintain higher degrees of independence changes along with the needs of the individual. It may be necessary for you to give the systems and gadgets you buy top priority, or you may want to think about purchasing them used or from eBay. Getting advice from a qualified occupational therapist will assist you in making the best decision for you and your loved one.

Chapter 6: Understanding Aggressively Violent Dementia

Alzheimer's patients can act out for no apparent cause. They could be quickly agitated or furious. They might yell, swear, or throw insults. They may even toss objects or push and punch caretakers in an attempt to get away from them. When a person reaches the later stages of the illness, this type of violence typically begins.

Nobody is certain why it occurs. It's possible that Alzheimer's disease itself causes aggression. It could also be an outward manifestation of confusion or frustration.

Recall that your loved one is not acting intentionally when they become aggressive. Additionally, there are things you can do to soothe them and prevent tantrums.

Recognize the triggers.

Aggression related to Alzheimer's might strike suddenly. There might not be a clear reason. However, triggers are frequently identifiable either before or during an issue.

Typical ones consist of:
Discomfort brought on by little sleep, adverse drug reactions, or inexplicable pain
The surroundings, such as commotion, excessive activity, or loud noises
Feeling stressed out by caregivers, attempting to grasp complicated instructions, or being asked too many questions at once can all cause confusion.
being touched or sensing that their personal space was violated—for example, when taking a shower or getting dressed.
observing your rage.

Being chastised or informed they were incorrect

Being hurried

being prohibited from doing something or going somewhere.

being forced to perform an unpleasant task

Sensing danger

Uncertainty about the situation

Believing that something was going on that wasn't real (for instance, being falsely accused of crimes like stealing or having an affair)

Could the aggressiveness be attributed to changes in habits or their surroundings? As an illustration:

Was the room they were in noisy?
Were they surrounded by numerous strangers?

Is drug or alcohol abuse a contributing factor to the issue?

Had something changed from their usual routine?

Could they be responding to your stress or feelings, such as annoyance or rage, by changing the way you look or speak?

Did their garments cause them any discomfort?

Was the space completely dark?

Could their physical sensations be the cause?

Do they exhibit symptoms of depression, such as eating, sleeping, or neither, and display little interest in everyday activities?

Do they feel any pain?

Could they be feeling under the weather?

They can be thirsty, hungry, cold, exhausted, or in need of the restroom.

6.1: Triggers and Risk Factors

One of the biggest sources of stress for nurses working in nursing homes is the sad prevalence of aggressive conduct in dementia patients. But it will be simple to control and even stop aggressive behavior once you know what sets it off.

Verbal forms of aggression include calling names, using derogatory language, yelling, and screaming. Alternative forms of abuse include shoving, hitting, punching, inappropriate touching, and even stabbing.

Aggression-causing factors

There's generally a reason why aggression occurs. Aggression is frequently sparked by the following in dementia patients:

Environmental factor: An individual with dementia may become overwhelmed or overstimulated in a noisy, crowded, dark, bright, chilly, hot, or overstimulating room, leading them to lash out in frustration.

Health factors: they typically make a dementia sufferer physically uncomfortable. The health factors could be sadness, ear or eye issues, pain, or infection (such as a urinary infection).

Ineffective communication: Dementia patients get hostile when they are unable to hear or comprehend what a nurse is saying.

Controlling hostility

Examine the surroundings: get rid of any elements that could be contributing to the hostility, such as brightening the space, lowering the noise level, or changing the temperature.

Employ the tactic of distraction: divert their attention with something enjoyable, such as watching television, taking a stroll, or listening to music. Additionally, this arouses their senses.

Medical examination: Take advantage of the moment when the combative individual settles down to examine them medically. Make an appointment with a doctor regardless of the health aspect to rule out any potential connections between it and their aggressive behavior.

Effective communication involves listening to the person with dementia, communicating in a calm manner to calm down an angry patient, using basic language, and providing clear, step-by-step instructions so that the person with dementia understands what needs to be done.

Pharmacological technique: If a patient with dementia

is endangering the safety of the nurses and other residents, pharmacology should be the last resort. To avoid pharmaceutical tolerance, it is advised against using medications to control aggression.

Staff nurses: you are never alone; you can always seek help from your peers. Reporting aggressiveness is also important, and you should let other nurses know about your experiences with it. You'll be able to learn from this how previous nurses handled similar situations. Nurses should remain composed and maintain a safe distance in the event of hostility.

Nurses will be better equipped to handle aggressiveness when it does arise by having a better understanding of the factors that contribute to violence. The patient-nurse connection improves when aggression in dementia patients is managed and prevented, and job pressures for nurses are avoided.

6.2: Assessing Violent Behaviors

It has long been the responsibility of the forensic psychology and psychiatric fields to comprehend the factors that contribute to aggression and offer assessments of a person's propensity for violent behavior.

Violent acts can be sexual, psychological, physical, or any mix of these. It is an intentional act of injury to another person. Over the previous two to three decades, there has undoubtedly been a shift in our understanding of the variables that lead to violence. And because of this, the development of risk assessment techniques has helped us become better at predicting the likelihood that someone will act out violently. However, the majority of the instruments now in use to help predict violence are primarily meant for young people and adults in the workforce who are involved in the criminal system. There are currently no instruments available to evaluate the threat of violence that older people pose.

Age, or age at the first violent event, is a primary risk factor found in most, if not all, violence risk assessment instruments. It is often known that young adults and adolescents are the age groups most likely to exhibit violent behavior.

The complex interplay between external factors—like unfavorable childhood experiences, inconsistent or strict parenting, early exposure to violence, and unfavorable peer associations—and individual factors—like poor emotion regulation, impulsivity, inadequate coping mechanisms, and inadequate problem-solving abilities—is cited as one of the reasons for this.

The risk field has also found that many of these problems lessen and the likelihood of violence decreases as we get older and reach mid-adulthood. Age and entering one's 60s have been found to gradually reduce an individual's probability of recidivism for specific types of violence (sexual violence in particular).

If so, how do we explain the acts of physical and sexual abuse that older people in their 70s and 80s have committed? We contend that because the population is getting older in many parts of the world, the science of risk assessment has to focus more attention and research on this particular age group.

Although violence has traditionally been linked to younger people, research on older people indicates that this is not just a problem for young people.

Studies carried out in long-term care environments emphasize the need for better techniques for risk assessment and management with senior citizens. In recent research, ninety percent of employees in 57 long-term care institutions said they had experienced abuse and harassment on a regular basis.

The majority of female health care workers claimed that they were subjected to verbal, sexual, and physical abuse so frequently that it had "normalized" in their workplaces.

Apart from the aggressiveness aimed at medical personnel, aggressive behavior among residents has also been a noteworthy issue in extended-care environments.

Elderly people who exhibit interpersonal aggression are not just found in long-term care facilities; intimate relationships have also been linked to this problem.

One may make the case that IPV perpetration is probably a life-course issue, meaning that individuals who committed IPV as working-aged adults will probably continue to act aggressively toward their intimate partners as they get older. On the other hand, not much is known about how this behavior developed. The studies on older people who have not had a history of hostility or interpersonal violence are even more lacking.

It is unclear what factors influence older individuals' interpersonal aggression. The same is probably true for older individuals, much like the interaction of internal and environmental risk factors that fuels aggression in youth and working-age adults. But the particular causes of violence in older people are probably very different.

The effects of aging on the brain as well as the particular psychosocial stresses that older persons face—such as diminished physical mobility, loss of significant others, and independence—must be taken into account.

It is also important to take into account the behavior exhibited over the course of a person's life: do people who have always been aggressive still act aggressively as they get older?

The influence of aging on cognition is one important risk factor that has been well documented. About 40% of us will have some memory problems as we get older, and for some of us, working memory, processing speed, and executive control will all deteriorate as we approach our senior years.

The alterations that occur naturally are much amplified in those who have dementia. It has been suggested that one of the main risk factors for older people committing acts of aggression is an impairment in executive functioning.

It is unclear, nevertheless, if the demyelination that comes with aging and dementia is related to aggression or if disinhibition brought on by injury or atrophy of various brain regions is to blame. More specifically, may this behavior be similar to the disinhibition associated with frontal impairment in cases of acute or chronic brain injury?

Aside from environmental stressors (such as being overstimulated or the time of day), social disengagement, fear, communication issues (such as having trouble using both receptive and expressive language), and physical discomfort, other factors that contribute to aggression in older people include fear.

Although individuals in the profession have recognized these aspects, it doesn't seem like a methodical approach has been made to comprehend risk factors that escalate or even ones that protect this group.

Currently, there is a lack of clarity regarding the consistent profile of individuals who get more aggressive with age. Is it feasible that as we investigate this topic, distinct typologies—that is, people that exhibit aggressive behavior throughout their lives—will surface?

Who are the aggressors—older persons who act aggressively but do not have severe cognitive impairment, or those who act aggressively because they have dementia or cognitive decline? And what part do medical co-morbidities (such as substance abuse, diabetes, and hypertension) play within each of these categories? If it is possible to distinguish between these typologies, what variables increase risk, what mitigating factors surface, and how do we handle the risk that is evident? Furthermore, a growing number of medical diseases are present in older people, and these conditions come with a variety of medications.

Numerous drugs have cognitive side effects, and polypharmacy can result in drug combinations that exacerbate cognitive or even impulse control issues.
There are currently just a few methods for managing the risk of violence and no age-specific risk assessment tools to help with risk assessments in the older adult population. Regarding the latter, there is a paucity of particular research on the use of drugs to lessen violence in older people, despite the fact that drugs are frequently used to manage challenging behaviors.

Actually, there is some evidence that some drugs may actually make people more aggressive. Certain antidepressants have been found to promote agitation and aggression, while benzodiazepines are known to cause paradoxical reactions of aggression and irritability in certain individuals. Although behavioral and psychological approaches have shown some promise in decreasing aggression, there is contention that a more comprehensive comprehension of risk and its contributing elements would guarantee that the variables influencing risk are suitably tackled.

All of this lends credence to the claim that, as the population ages, it will be more important than ever for the risk assessment community and the healthcare system to focus on this particular group.

Chapter 7: Coping with Caregiver Stress

High levels of stress are often reported by caregivers for Alzheimer's patients. Taking care of a loved one who has Alzheimer's or any dementia can be extremely taxing, but too much stress can be detrimental to you both. Learn about the signs of burnout and prevent it by reading on.

Signs of stress in caregivers

1. A denial of the illness and how it affects the individual with the diagnosis. I have faith that Mom will recover.

2. Resentment toward the Alzheimer's patient or annoyance that they are unable to perform the activities

they formerly could.

He's only being obstinate; he understands how to get dressed.

3. Withdrawing socially from acquaintances and past enjoyable pursuits.
Visiting with the neighbors no longer interests me.

4. Fear of the future and starting a new day.
What happens if I'm not able to provide him the care he needs?

5. Depression that destroys your soul and impairs your capacity for adjustment.
I simply no longer give a damn.

6. Such exhaustion that it is almost impossible to carry out daily chores. I'm too worn out to do this.

7. Lack of sleep brought on by an endless to-do list of worries.

What happens if she gets lost in the house or trips and falls and gets hurt?

8. Irritability that sets off unpleasant reactions and behaviors and makes one moody. Give me some space!

9. A lack of focus that causes difficulties doing routine chores.

I overlooked my appointment since I was so busy.

10. health issues that start to affect one's physical and emotional well-being.

When was the last time I felt well?

Make time to speak with your doctor if you frequently suffer from any of these symptoms of stress.

Strategies for stress management

See your physician if you frequently exhibit symptoms of stress. You run the risk of losing your bodily and mental well-being if you ignore symptoms.

Make use of calming strategies.

Stress relief is possible using a number of relaxing methods. To determine which one suits you the best, try a few. Methods consist of:
Mentally imagining a serene and tranquil environment or circumstance is known as visualization.

Meditation (which is as easy as setting aside 15 minutes a day to let go of all ideas that are stressful)
Breathing exercises: slow down and concentrate on inhaling deeply.
Progressive muscle relaxation is the process of first tightening and then relaxing each muscle group in your body, beginning at one end and moving towards the other.

Get in motion.

Any kind of physical activity can help lower stress and enhance general wellbeing. 10 minutes a day of exercise can make a difference. Go for a stroll. Engage in a hobby or pastime you enjoy, like dancing or gardening.

Make time for yourself.

To free up time for activities you enjoy, think about utilizing respite care. While the Alzheimer's patient receives care in a secure setting, caregivers can take a brief break from providing care thanks to respite care. Find out more about short-term care.

Develop into an informed caregiver.

It could be important to acquire new caregiving skills as the illness worsens. Programs are available from the Alzheimer's Association to assist you in comprehending and managing the behavioral and personality changes that frequently accompany Alzheimer's disease. Speaking with other caregivers and care partners about how they are handling the difficulties brought on by the illness and uncertainty about the future may also be beneficial.

Attend to your own needs.

See your physician on a regular basis. Aim for a healthy diet, regular exercise, and lots of sleep. Maintaining your health might make you a more effective caregiver.

Keep your comedy in check.

Maintaining your sense of humor does not imply trivializing or mocking the circumstances. Laughter is a useful coping mechanism. Comedian and celebrity champion Chris Garcia talks about how comedy supported him and his family during his father's Alzheimer's disease. His father was a Cuban exile.

Plan your finances and legal matters.

After receiving an Alzheimer's diagnosis, it's critical to set up financial and legal arrangements so that the affected individual can take part. Making plans for the future might give the family peace of mind. It is possible to prepare many documents without an attorney's assistance. But you might want to get help from an elder law attorney, a financial advisor experienced in elder or long-term care planning, or both if you are unclear about how to fill out legal paperwork or establish financial preparations. Study up on forward planning.

7.1: Recognizing Burnout

While providing much-needed love and comfort to a loved one might sometimes make you feel happy and energetic, there are other times when caring for a loved one can be overpowering and show up as exhaustion, tension, anxiety, or despair. We call this "caregiver burnout" in the community of caregivers. It's important to maintain your physical, emotional, and mental wellness in order to give your loved one the best care possible. Burnout and exhaustion are normal emotions experienced by caregivers on a daily basis.

Are you trying to find ways to keep caregivers from burning out? Below, we've listed our top seven suggestions:

Put it in writing: Have you ever had a blue mood yet been unable to identify the cause? Or perhaps you've been extremely frustrated and haven't had anywhere to let it out? It has been discovered that journaling significantly improves mental and emotional health. Writing down your ideas compels your brain to work through your emotions and frustrations as you express them. The act of journaling is frequently relieving because, over time, putting your issues down in writing can help them seem more controllable or even unimportant. Don't bother about punctuation, grammar, or even writing entire phrases when you're journaling.

Simply start your entry with "Today I feel..." and then write whatever comes to mind.

Permit Yourself to Experience Negative Feelings: Providing care for others won't always be easy. Even though a lot of caretakers hope that their presence will always improve the health of their loved ones, it isn't always possible. Additionally, you need to understand that this is an unreasonable expectation if your loved one has a degenerative illness like dementia or Alzheimer's disease. Let your anger, tension, or resentment out and learn healthy ways to channel your negative emotions instead of holding them inside, which exacerbates caregiver burnout.

Recognize your boundaries; you are not a superman. It is impossible to perform flawlessly every day. Periodically checking in with oneself helps you remember that it's acceptable to face obstacles or feel worn out from work. Never assume that you can't make time for yourself because you're too busy taking care of someone else. Give yourself personal time to unwind, even if it's just for fifteen minutes, thirty minutes, or an hour. A quick and easy way to reduce stress is to practice deep breathing or meditation. These techniques can improve your mental health throughout the day.

Seek Patterns: What aspects of your role in providing care cause you to feel stressed, anxious, or depressed? Does anything specific happen every day that triggers your bad emotions? Understanding what sets off your feelings of caregiver burnout gives you valuable information to help keep them from happening again in the future. You may plan ahead for—or perhaps prevent—caregiver burnout episodes by identifying what triggers them.

Read a Book: To assist caregivers on their journey, our support groups have identified several excellent caregiver novels. These publications offer much-needed guidance on how to maintain the appeal, manageability, and satisfaction of providing care.

Benefit from Respite Care: Respite care enables caregivers to take a break from their caring responsibilities by employing a qualified individual to fill in for them temporarily. This break gives caregivers much-needed "me time" to attend to personal matters such as traveling, attending appointments, or engaging in social events.

7.2: Self-Care Strategies

A collection of disorders affecting the brain is called dementia. It can affect a person's attitude, actions, and most prevalent symptom, memory. Taking care of a loved one who has dementia can be incredibly taxing, and you can even face a number of mental and physical difficulties yourself.

Strategies for self-care by dementia caregivers

Continue to be physically healthy.

When you give someone all of your attention and resources, it might be easy to overlook your own health. Nonetheless, you may give your loved one the finest care possible if you take the time to look after your own health.

It's critical for caregivers to maintain a healthy, well-balanced diet, engage in regular exercise, and get enough sleep. The more confident you are in yourself, the more capable you are of taking care of others.

Observe your mental well-being.

Regrettably, a lot of unpaid caregivers have feelings of overload or overloading their caring responsibilities. When a loved one's personality starts to shift, some people may feel stressed, anxious, angry, depressed, resentful, or even grieve. The health of the individual receiving care as well as the caregiver themselves may suffer from excessive stress and anxiety. It is crucial that you avoid overworking yourself as a result.

Take time for your own happiness, objectives, and purposes if your caregiving role is compromising your mental health. It is best to accept your emotions and to seek support from friends or a professional counseling agency when necessary. The most crucial thing to keep in mind is that there are a lot of support systems available, and you are not alone.

Take a rest.

If you are a full-time caregiver, it is tempting to set unrealistic expectations for yourself. But creating a well-balanced lifestyle can be greatly enhanced by taking breaks from your care responsibilities to enjoy your own life. Make an effort to plan enough downtime so that you can completely relax, recharge, get some sleep, and even treat yourself. You're worthy of it!

With the help of our respite care service, you may take the time you need to regroup and return to your caring position feeling fully prepared to offer your all. Recall that taking care of your own health and wellness is just as vital as looking after the health and welfare of your loved ones.

Create a solid support system.

Having a strong support system can be crucial for overcoming difficult circumstances. Make an effort to stay in touch with loved ones who are willing to lend you a shoulder and an ear. You might even want to consider joining a support group for caregivers, where you can talk about your experiences and get and provide advice from others who are in similar situations.

Certain family caregivers may qualify for government-funded assistance to provide them with financial support while taking care of a loved one.

Chapter 8: Medical Treatments and Therapies

A medical professional must identify the pattern of skill and function loss in order to diagnose dementia. What the person is still capable of doing is also assessed by the care provider. Recently, biomarkers have been created to aid in more accurate Alzheimer's disease diagnosis.

A medical practitioner examines you physically and goes over your symptoms and medical history. Someone close to you may also inquire about your symptoms.

Dementia cannot be diagnosed by a single test. To find the problem, you probably need to run a few tests.

Tests of cognition and neuropsychology
These assessments gauge your capacity for thought. Thinking abilities, including memory, orientation,

judgment and reasoning, language proficiency, and attention, are measured by a variety of tests.

Neurological assessment

We assess your recall, linguistic proficiency, visual perception, focus, problem-solving abilities, movement, senses, balance, reflexes, and other areas.

Brain imaging

CT or MRI scans can be used to look for signs of hydrocephalus, a buildup of fluid in the brain, hemorrhage, stroke, or tumors.

PET scans: These scans are able to display brain activity patterns. They are able to ascertain whether the brain has been exposed to amyloid or tau proteins, which are indicators of Alzheimer's disease.

Lab examinations

Basic blood tests can identify medical conditions like low vitamin B-12 levels or underactive thyroid glands that might impair brain function. Occasionally, the spinal fluid is tested for inflammation, infection, or signs of certain degenerative illnesses.

Psychiatric assessment

Your symptoms can be evaluated by a mental health specialist to see if depression or another mental illness is the cause.

Lab examinations

Basic blood tests can identify medical conditions like low vitamin B-12 levels or underactive thyroid glands that might impair brain function. Occasionally, the spinal fluid is tested for inflammation, infection, or signs of certain degenerative illnesses.

Handling

While there isn't a treatment for the majority of dementias, there are strategies to control your symptoms.

Drugs

The following are methods for momentarily alleviating the symptoms of dementia.

Cholinesterase inhibitors: These medications function by increasing the body's supply of a chemical messenger that is important for judgment and memory. Among these are galantamine (Razadyne ER), rivastigmine (Exelon), and donepezil (Aricept, Adlarity).

These medications may also be used for other dementias, even though their main purpose is the treatment of Alzheimer's disease. People with Lewy body dementia, Parkinson's disease dementia, and vascular dementia may be prescribed them.

Digestion, vomiting, and nausea are possible side effects. Slower heart rate, fainting, and difficulty sleeping are further potential adverse effects.

Memantine: Memantine (Namenda) functions by controlling glutamate's action. Glutamate is another chemical messenger that plays a role in memory and learning in the brain. Memantine may occasionally be administered in combination with a cholinesterase inhibitor.

Dizziness is a frequent adverse effect of memantine.

Additional medications: To address symptoms or other diseases, you may take additional medications. Treatment may be necessary for agitation, hallucinations, depression, sleep issues, or parkinsonism.

Lecanemab, also known as Leqembi, was approved by

the U.S. Food and Drug Administration (FDA) in 2023 for use in treating moderate Alzheimer's disease and mild cognitive impairment.

People with early Alzheimer's disease showed less cognitive deterioration when using the medication, according to phase 3 clinical research. The medication keeps amyloid plaques from sticking together in the brain. The phase 3 experiment was the biggest to date, investigating the possibility of delaying the disease by removing amyloid plaque clusters from the brain.

Every two weeks, an IV injection of lecanemab is administered. Lecanemab side effects include reactions associated with the infusion, including fever, flu-like symptoms, nausea, vomiting, disorientation, altered heart rate, and dyspnea.

Individuals using lecanemab may also experience cerebral edema or minor hemorrhages. On rare occasions, cerebral edema may become so severe as to induce seizures and other symptoms. Bleeding in the brain can also occasionally result in death. The FDA advises obtaining a brain MRI prior to beginning any kind of treatment. Additionally, it suggests having brain MRIs performed while receiving treatment to check for signs of brain hemorrhage or edema.

Individuals who possess the APOE e4 gene variant seem to be more susceptible to these dangerous side effects. Prior to beginning lecanemab medication, the FDA advises being tested for this gene.

Consult your healthcare provider before using lecanemab if you have any other risk factors for brain bleeding or if you take blood thinners. Medication that thins the blood may make brain bleeding more likely.

The possible dangers of using lecanemab are the subject of additional research. Further studies are examining the potential efficacy of lecanemab for those at risk of Alzheimer's disease, including those who have a first-degree family member, like a parent or sibling, who has the condition.

Donanemab is another medication under investigation. It targets tau proteins and amyloid plaques, reducing them. It has been observed to lessen cognitive and functional deterioration in individuals with early-stage Alzheimer's disease.

Treatments

A number of behavioral issues and dementia symptoms may be first managed with techniques other than medication. These could consist of:

Occupational therapy: An occupational therapist can teach you coping mechanisms and demonstrate how to make your house safer. The intention is to stop mishaps like falls. In addition to helping you control your behavior, therapy gets you ready for when the dementia gets worse.

Adjustments to the surroundings: A person suffering from dementia may find it easier to concentrate and operate if there is less noise and clutter. Knives and car keys are two examples of items you may need to conceal. You can be informed by monitoring systems if the dementia patient wanders.

Easier chores: It can be beneficial to divide activities into manageable pieces and concentrate on achievement rather than failure. Regularity and structure aid in lowering confusion in dementia patients.

Talking with your loved one about their hometown, school days, career, or favorite pastimes can all be part of reminiscence therapy. It can be carried out in groups or one-on-one settings as a component of formal therapy.

The facilitator may include mementos like old photographs or other objects from your loved one's life in addition to music from their past.

An organized program called cognitive stimulation therapy (CST) is used with groups of individuals who have mild to moderate dementia. During meetings, the group does mentally taxing activities like singing, word games, cooking from a recipe, and discussing current events.

Basic information, including the person's name, the date, and the time, is covered in reality orientation training. They may have posted signs all throughout their house with such information. This is too much for some people, or perhaps perceived as condescending. Give it up if your loved one isn't benefiting from it.

8.1: Drugs for Treating Illnesses

While there are currently no drugs that can prevent, delay, or reverse dementia, some can improve a person's thinking and memory for a short while.

Four drugs have been approved to help people with dementia symptoms, such as memory and cognitive issues:

Galantamine, memantine, rivastigmine, and donepezil.

Only those with Alzheimer's disease, dementia with Lewy bodies, dementia from Parkinson's disease, and mixed dementia, including any combination of these conditions, can benefit from these treatments.

Currently, there are no drugs that alleviate the symptoms of frontotemporal dementia or vascular dementia. But drugs should never be the only thing keeping you hopeful. A person's ability to live well can be enhanced by activities, social support, non-pharmacological therapies, information, and guidance.

Varieties of dementia drugs

There are at least two names for many dementia medications:

A term for the active ingredient in the drug, such as donepezil

A trademark, like Aricept.

Slow-release capsules: these form a slow release of the drug into the body. When consumed, regular pills and capsules release the drug into the body.

How do these drugs for dementia function?

Galantamine, rivastigmine, and donepezil
Naturally occurring substances in a healthy brain facilitate communication between nerve cells. Acetylcholine is one of these compounds. A person with Lewy body dementia or Alzheimer's disease has lower levels of acetylcholine in their bodies. This implies that their nerve cells are unable to communicate with each other correctly.

Acetylcholine levels can be increased by cholinesterase inhibitors such as galantamine, rivastigmine, and donepezil. This prolongs the duration of regular brain function. While all three cholinesterase inhibitors function similarly, some people may respond better to one than the other. One may experience fewer adverse effects, for example.

The illness will eventually cause enough brain damage that these drugs will no longer have as much of an impact. The patient's symptoms will start to worsen once more at this point.

All three drugs—galantamine, rivastigmine, and donepezil—belong to a class of drugs known as cholinesterase inhibitors and function similarly. Memantine functions in a unique way.

Memantine for Alzheimer's

Memantine functions differently from the other drugs. Glutamate overdosing is a possible symptom of Alzheimer's disease. Their ability to transmit messages is hampered by this injury to their nerve cells. Memantine inhibits glutamate, which safeguards a person's nerve cells.

To whom are dementia treatments beneficial?

Certain people benefit more than others from memory and cognitive medications. Those with Alzheimer's disease who have taken a cholinesterase inhibitor for six months are participating in clinical trials.

Eight out of ten people won't notice a difference, while roughly one out of ten will clearly see an improvement in their memory and thinking. Roughly one out of ten people will have negative side effects.

Clinical trials addressing individuals with Parkinson's disease dementia or dementia with Lewy bodies have been less common. Nonetheless, data suggests that these illnesses benefit more from cholinesterase inhibitor drugs than from Alzheimer's disease.

Rivastigmine with donepezil

The most widely prescribed drug for dementia treatment is, without a doubt, donepezil. When donepezil creates side effects or a patient cannot take it for medical reasons, rivastigmine is typically the only medication utilized.

Advantages

Quantity

When should someone take galantamine?

Seldom is galantamine administered. It can be applied to alleviate Alzheimer's disease symptoms. Doctors, however, are more likely to start with rivastigmine and donepezil.

The effectiveness of galantamine in treating Lewy body or Parkinson's disease dementia is unknown.

Quantity

Typically, a galantamine user would begin by taking two 4 mg capsules each day with breakfast and dinner. After that, the dosage can be raised every few weeks to a daily maximum of 24 mg. A slow-release form of galantamine is also offered, which may lessen adverse effects.

When should I get memantine prescribed?

Memantine is used to treat patients with Lewy body dementia or Alzheimer's disease in the middle and later phases of the illness. It can assist with declining mental capacities, such as disorientation, and difficulties performing everyday tasks, such as putting on clothes.

There is some evidence to suggest that memantine can occasionally help with agitation, violence, and delusions.

A cholinesterase inhibitor alone may not always be as helpful as memantine for someone with late-stage Alzheimer's disease. This can be a result of the medications' various modes of action.

Quantity

When starting memantine, it is typical to receive a "starter pack." This has a range of strengths in the pills, so over a few weeks, they can build up to an effective dose. They begin at a modest dose of 5 mg per day and increase by 5 mg each week until, after four weeks, they are taking 20 mg per day.

8.2: Non-Medical Interventions

Non-pharmacological is just a fancy way of saying non-medical. For your loved one, non-pharmacological dementia interventions like employing a research-based design that promotes independence might be the best course of action. The application of programming that makes use of social, physical, intellectual, and nutritional involvement is another illustration of a non-pharmacological method. While many pharmacological (medical) interventions concentrate on treating symptoms, non-pharmacological interventions frequently treat the whole person. Non-pharmacological therapies have been shown in studies to significantly improve cognitive function, independence, and quality of life in people with dementia while also causing sustainable gains. Furthermore, they might enhance fine motor abilities, physical functionality, neuroplasticity, and even vision. Dementia symptoms can often be slowed down if a person participates in regular social, physical, intellectual, and nutritional activities.

Although there is presently no cure for the majority of dementia types, there are treatment options available, including both pharmaceutical and non-pharmacological methods and interventions. Regrettably, there are false beliefs about pharmaceutical care. A common misconception is that drugs used to treat dementia symptoms really slow down the disease's progression. Medications, such as decongestants, can relieve congestion but not the flu; they are merely a temporary cover for the symptoms.

That being said, non-pharmacological intervention can significantly improve a dementia patient's quality of life.

In the treatment of dementia, non-pharmacological therapies include:

1. Refrain from using black doormats or welcome mats since someone suffering from dementia can mistake them for a hole.

2. Play therapeutic music to promote socializing and boost vitality.

3. Apply clinical aromatherapy, which can enhance focus and involvement.

4. Incorporate light therapy, which can promote a healthy circadian rhythm—our body's natural rhythm connected to our sleep cycle.

Chapter 9: Engaging Activities and Social Connections

We all know that socializing with others is good for people with dementia, but the real question is, what kinds of fun things can they do specifically? It has been demonstrated that singing, listening to music, and browsing through old photo albums can all help alleviate symptoms. Certain brain regions may be stimulated by them in relation to memories. Playing games is even more enjoyable. People with dementia have more and more gaming possibilities as technology develops.

Video Games Those who wouldn't typically be interested in gaming are increasingly able to access easy-to-play video games on the iPad or other tablets. Playing on a tablet is one of the evidence-based activities that can help people with dementia with their executive functioning. This covers tasks like planning and organizing.

Consider, for a moment, a video game that revolves around cooking. As players imitate duties related to cooking, various brain areas are stimulated during gameplay. According to studies, playing video games improved cognitive function in those with Alzheimer's and moderate cognitive impairment.

Other games that benefit those suffering from dementia are:

Cognifit. After evaluating your memory and other cognitive abilities, this game offers easy games to help strengthen particular brain regions.

- Companion. This game mixes workouts, videos, and recipes with games.

More applications are appropriate for those suffering from dementia. Video games that are usually thought of as kid-friendly can benefit senior citizens suffering from dementia. Players can take turns imitating the gestures for sports like tennis and bowling on devices like the Xbox Kinect and Nintendo Wii. It has been shown that these movements, simplicity, and one-turn-at-a-time gameplay style help people with cognitive impairment become more independent and capable learners.

Puzzles and board games

Although board games may appear too challenging for someone suffering from dementia, they actually have the potential to enhance cognitive abilities. According to one study, dementia patients who played bingo on a regular basis performed better on naming and identification tests. You may buy bingo games to play at home, and there are even free tablet apps available for playing online bingo. Go out into the neighborhood and play a game of bingo with other senior citizens if your loved one is in the early stages of Alzheimer's disease or a related dementia.

There are a ton of additional tabletop games available that are suitable for dementia sufferers. choosing a piece with vibrant boards and components—especially larger, manageable ones. Try dominoes, checkers, or chutes and ladders. Playing basic card games with someone who has dementia can also be enjoyable, such as war and blackjack. If your loved one has trouble seeing playing cards, you can consider getting them large-print cards.

Another excellent option is a jigsaw puzzle, particularly one with fewer than 500 pieces. Remind yourself to ease this on your loved one and make sure all the parts are there before starting.

9.1: Meaningful Activities for Individuals with Dementia

Keeping up worthwhile activities enhances the worth and quality of a person's life, regardless of whether they have been diagnosed with dementia. Depending on the stage of dementia at which a person is diagnosed, their skills and talents will differ significantly. We can ensure that the needs of the person with dementia are satisfied not just when their condition worsens but even in the current epidemic, which has caused a large number of people to stay indoors, by trying to come up with activities that provide them with as much purpose and engagement as possible.

Engaging activities like a call or a Zoom session with family or friends can be considered meaningful activities, as can routine daily chores like cooking, cleaning, gardening, and self-care.

In order to help those who are living with dementia lead healthier and more pleasurable lives, it is crucial to try and retain those interests and relationships. Dementia can cause people to withdraw from hobbies and enjoyable interactions with family. Individuals with dementia may exhibit apathetic behaviors and withdraw, such as nodding off at odd hours or getting easily sidetracked. This can occasionally make interacting with the dementia patient challenging.

Relevant activities ought to be connected to interests or pastimes the person had before being diagnosed with dementia. When it is feasible, it is best to let the person suffering from dementia choose and define the activities that have importance for them. This will make it easier to make sure that interactions are formed and sustained and that the activity has significance.

modifying tasks as the dementia worsens

Depending on a person's physical capabilities, the level of dementia they are in, and the range of supports available to them—including whether they live alone or have family members who can care for them—adaptation and adaptations to activities may be required. People who have dementia should participate in family activities as much as possible. If the correct meaningful activities are followed, there's no reason this can't happen in the wake of the pandemic, with more families choosing to spend time indoors.

All things considered, meaningful activity gives the dementia sufferer:

Routine and a sense of purpose.

Acknowledges and makes use of the dementia patient's abilities and experiences.

Emotionally nourishing events that boost a person's confidence and make them feel important.

Possibility of spending more time with family socially

Preserve autonomy and abilities, and in certain situations, enhance the person's capacity to carry out specific everyday tasks.

The ability to choose and make decisions.

9.2: Connecting with Community Resources

After learning that you or a loved one has dementia, you must act quickly to locate local resources for dementia care services.

There are various places to go to gain information on dementia and your next steps, from websites and online resources to local groups that specialize in dementia care and family support.

Vice president for education at the James L. West Center for Dementia Care, Jaime Cobb Tinsley, stated, "It's easy to be overwhelmed when you or your loved one receives a dementia diagnosis." You won't need assistance right away, but you don't have to figure everything out right away. Spend some time studying and researching.

Family members are frequently unaware of their own ignorance. When you don't know what the questions are yet, it can be challenging to know what to ask.

For almost thirty years, James L. West has provided residential care, day programs for people with dementia, and education to the Fort Worth dementia community.

Families with recently diagnosed loved ones often contact the team with inquiries.

Locating local options for people suffering from dementia

Alzheimer's Associations, Area Agencies on Aging in your area, and other community organizations that specialize in dementia care are excellent places to start when searching for local services for patients with dementia.

Area Organization on Aging There are 28 area agencies in Texas, and North Central Texas is one of 670 throughout the US. These neighborhood groups run programs that help caregivers at home, including financial aid for respite care, support groups, and education.

Alzheimer-Friendly An additional resource to assist caregivers in connecting with services to support caregiving at home is Fort Worth, a local group dedicated to creating a community that respects, appreciates, supports, and includes people living with dementia. They provide weekly "memory cafés" and online engagement activities for people with dementia and their caregivers.

For families and care partners, James L. West provides free online and in-person classes on dementia and caregiving. The James L. West website and YouTube channel offer recorded and on-demand access to their online sessions.

There are thousands of results when searching Google for dementia or Alzheimer's dementia, but not all of these sources of information are reliable.

The National Institute on Aging, the National Institutes of Health, and the Alzheimer's Association all have webpages that the James L. West team suggests checking out. There is a lot of information on the illness and its symptoms available on these websites. Resources for both the dementia patient and the caregiver are available on the Alzheimer's Association website.

Regarding Alzheimer's disease and other types of dementia, trustworthy resources include the Alzheimer's Foundation of America and the Mayo Clinic. On the website of the Alzheimer's Foundation of America, you can locate respectable member groups committed to enhancing the quality of life for individuals diagnosed with dementia.

According to Skinner, "there's so much good information out there." However, a lot of false information is also available. It's wise to verify anything you find by consulting a reliable source, such as a medical professional or your primary care physician. On the Internet, not everything is true.

Caregivers with dementia: support groups
Taking care of oneself first is the best thing a caregiver can do for a loved one suffering from dementia. Attending a support group for dementia caregivers improves mental health and reduces stress.

It's crucial to find a support group as soon as possible, and there are plenty to pick from, both offline and online.

The James L. West Center and the local branch of the Alzheimer's Association are two of the Fort Worth organizations that provide support groups for those caring for a loved one with dementia. There are both online and in-person support groups accessible.

Support groups for caregivers of dementia patients offer a secure setting for caregivers to connect and exchange stories about their experiences. Professionally facilitated, these groups enable caregivers to support one another through the highs and lows of caring for a loved one with dementia.

According to Skinner, utilizing Facebook's search function to find dementia support groups is a simple way to find them on the social media site.

Cobb Tinsley stated, "There are online support groups that are very helpful and groups that are not so helpful." "It's OK to look for another group that is more beneficial to your situation if you're in an online group that you don't find helpful."

Tools to increase in-home care provision

For as long as possible, many caregivers desire to maintain their loved ones at home. They will require different community resources as their loved one's dementia worsens. Lists of local providers are kept up to date by the Alzheimer's Association and Area Agencies on Aging.

Home health agencies are a Medicare and/or Medicaid-funded service that can help short-term patients with physical, occupational, and speech therapy as well as everyday life skills like washing and grooming.

Numerous for-profit home care organizations are available to offer in-home services like companionship and assistance with everyday life activities like dressing, bathing, and housework. In certain circumstances, long-term care insurance may also cover this service, which is offered at an hourly or daily cost. If you look for personal assistance or home care services in your area, you'll find a lot of providers.

"Respite services can even be performed in your home at night," stated Hollie Glover, the director of family support and education. "That's very crucial during the intermediate stages, when they might get up and move around or do something risky."

An adult day program is an additional choice for assistance in providing care for a dementia patient. This is a drop-off program that provides care for the dementia patient while the caregiver takes a vacation. Helping someone successfully get care at home is a fantastic service.

For more than thirty years, the James L. West Senior Day Program has provided care for those suffering from dementia. This program is offered from 7:30 a.m. to 6 p.m., Monday through Friday. The day program offers medicine administration and other nursing services, showering, hair and nail care, meals and snacks, and enjoyable, productive activities all day long, while the caregiver goes to work, takes a break, or takes care of their own needs.

Ensuring that the individual with dementia has an engaging day with like-minded others is crucial. We want them to have a happy, fulfilling day and to return home exhausted so they can have a good night's sleep every night. Day programs are far less expensive than placement. Day program care is covered by certain long-term care insurances. Moreover, day program services may be covered by certain veterans's benefits. Since James L. West is a non-profit day program, it provides scholarships to people who are unable to pay the daily fee.

Planning ahead for dementia patients' care
It's never too early to begin making arrangements for the

care that a loved one suffering from dementia might require.

Organize your finances first. It can be costly to care for a person with dementia, and it might take time to get approved for financial aid.

"Get on it now if you even suspect you could require Medicaid. Medicaid has a 60-month lookback period, according to Glover. "It is best to get started as soon as possible."

Medicaid specialists frequently work with elder attorneys and can help with the application process. To find out your choices if a loved one served in the military, get in touch with the Veterans Administration.

You will require the assistance of a social worker to manage the medical aspect of things. It's crucial to begin your search as soon as possible because there's frequently a three- to six-week wait to be assigned.

Creating advance care planning documentation is another crucial early action to take if your loved one is still able to give direction for their future medical care.

Chapter 10: Caregiver Experiences

It can be taxing to provide dementia care for someone.

According to the results of a recent AARP poll, people who look after loved ones who have dementia tend to work longer hours and require more life adaptations than people who look after people who have other medical illnesses.

The national survey examined the needs of 400 caregivers of a loved one without dementia and roughly 700 caregivers of people with dementia or other forms of cognitive impairment (usually their parents). In any case, caregivers say they have been taking care of their loved one for about three years on average.

The majority of poll results indicate that providing care for a person with dementia entails extra challenges, despite 75% of respondents saying it has given their lives more meaning. As an illustration:

The average weekly caring time for caregivers of dementia patients is 13.7 hours, compared to 11.7 hours for other caregivers.

The largest challenges of caring for someone with dementia, according to about 32% of caregivers, are managing emotions and the needs of care.

Respondents state that their health status is the same whether or not they provide care for a person with dementia; nevertheless, those who provide care for someone with dementia are more likely than non-caregivers to report that they have put off taking care of their own health needs—55 percent against only 38 percent among non-caregivers.

In addition, caregivers for individuals with dementia are more likely to state that providing care has resulted in decreased sleep, increased anxiety and sadness, less time spent alone and with friends, and feelings of loneliness. Additionally, a greater percentage of dementia caregivers than other caregivers (36%), almost 63%, claim that their caregiving responsibilities have caused them to work different hours, leave work early or unexpectedly, and worry about finances.

While two-thirds of caregivers overall say they feel closer to their loved one, caregivers of people with dementia are more likely than other caregivers (13%), to think their relationship has grown more distant over time (22%), than with their loved one. Caregivers of loved ones suffering from dementia are also more likely to report poor relationships with other family members.

Caregivers often report that they are getting what they require from medical professionals, but individuals who are taking care of someone who has dementia also look for more information about providing care from a wider range of sources.

10.1: Personal Stories of Caregiving Challenges

After receiving a dementia diagnosis, Tracey Clayton's aunt went through phases of disbelief and uncertainty. She now discusses the lessons she discovered along the way.

For nine years, Tracey was her aunt's primary caregiver.

When someone you care about initially has memory issues, you will likely try to find a logical reason for it.

I initially assumed that my aunt's forgetting our lunch meeting was the result of her being preoccupied. It grew strange when the same incident occurred twice. But my alarm really started to go off when she left the house with the stove still blazing. I finally made the decision to take her to the doctor.

Denunciation arrived first.

I was astounded and afraid of what awaited us when the results were in. When the doctor discussed Alzheimer's disease, its symptoms, development, and the necessity for ongoing treatment, her words seemed so disorganized in my mind. I made the decision to read as much as I could about this ailment as soon as I got home.

It might take a lot of time and effort to care for someone who has Alzheimer's or dementia. It takes a great deal of time, patience, and devotion. My aunt's functional, physical, and cognitive capacities started to deteriorate over time, making this situation worse.

It can be extremely stressful and even depressing to witness someone you love in that state, and it can be quite draining to put your own well-being and personal life on the back burner in order to care for them. Sometimes, your loved one will act like someone else entirely, and that can be really upsetting. It is crucial that you have support as well, whether it comes from friends, family, a partner, or even support groups.

Overcoming the obstacles

There are numerous difficulties that arise when caring for someone who has dementia or Alzheimer's disease. Every person's illness develops differently, so there isn't a set course of action that applies to everyone. While planning can be beneficial, there are always fresh obstacles to overcome.

I was able to overcome communication barriers with my aunt by speaking in plain terms and attempting to grab her attention before speaking. Bladder issues were also challenging, but they got simpler as we made it a habit to take her to the restroom.

The hardest aspect of the experience was the delusions and hallucinations, but it's crucial to try not to argue. Abrupt mood swings and violent outbursts require a great deal of tolerance and understanding.

An encounter that would change my life

Keeping your loved one safe and reducing their possibilities of straying off is the most crucial part of giving care. I made sure the main doors were locked, especially at night, and I provided my aunt with a piece of identification that had her address and phone number.

My aunt had Alzheimer's for nine years, and I had been her principal caregiver, witnessing her gradual decline. It goes without saying that I found this to be quite challenging, but I always made an effort to keep in mind that she also finds it challenging.

It's critical to understand that you won't leave this experience exactly as you were before. The fact that you were decent and compassionate to someone you love during such trying times should be enough of a reward, though, if you refuse to let the illness overtake you.

10.2: Lessons Learned and Advice from Experienced Caregivers

My beautiful, kind mother passed away two years ago. She was eighty-five years old.

Mom was still able to make high kicks while seated in her chair and touch her toes six months before she passed away! She had superb hand-eye coordination and occasionally had acute hearing. However, she was unable to speak to anyone anymore. She was unable to put words together to form a coherent phrase.

She had no idea who I was, but I believe she recognized that I was somebody she knew and could trust.

She continued to adore flowers. My dad and she both loved gardening, and he bought her flowers a lot.

She began to dislike the brightest, most colorful flowers as her dementia worsened and took away her ability to remember plant and flower names. Examples of these blooms are large, bold lilies, multicolored tulips, and artificially colored carnations.

She could smell them all the time. "Excellent," she

would remark. And she was a lovely spirit in and of
herself.

Observing Mum's dementia symptoms

A few years after my dad, her soul mate, passed away,
we initially observed slight deviations in Mum's
behavior and demeanor—nothing that would have been
noticeable to anybody outside of our immediate family.

Although Mum has always enjoyed assisting others,
particularly her elderly or lonely neighbors, their
dependence on her started to bother and burden her.

Although she had a strong sense of arithmetic, was adept
at handling her personal finances, and had an
outstanding recall, she began to make mistakes such as
buying extra food, paying for newspaper deliveries
weeks in advance, and forgetting to make tea for guests.

214

She gradually lost confidence in going outside the house and on public transportation.

Although she was always an excellent baker and cook, she began to overcook food and once burned toast because she didn't realize it was under the grill. She insisted on eating it after realizing what she had done, saying, "So [she] didn't do it again!" After that, she never used the cooker unattended.

Her cognitive abilities gradually eluded her. Once a voracious reader, she was unable to keep up with a novel and, oddly, kept buying them even though most of them went unread.

Word searches took the place of general knowledge crosswords, which she could complete at breakneck speed. She would read newspapers, but the stories would emotionally impact her. Her perception of television shifted from being an enjoyable diversion to one of distrust and terror, as she believed that the person she was watching was also observing her.

She acknowledged that she was changing, and I believe this made her feel both pleased and ashamed of herself. She had assisted in the care of her own mother, who had suffered from Alzheimer's for twenty years. However, she was unmoved to see her GP.

Urged to visit the doctor

Then, one year, while on a family vacation, she vanished from their hotel.

Early that morning, a kind stranger discovered her on a train platform and brought her to the nearby police station. Reluctantly, she went home after being advised that she needed to see her general practitioner. "They think I'm daft," she wrote in her diary.

Her Alzheimer's diagnosis marked the start of our family's educational and enlightening journey. Every member of the family and I had to figure out how to deal with the adjustments, annoyances, fears, and losses that this illness causes.

It felt at times like we were marching through deep, shifting sands with the hope of never finding the oasis that would heal us!

In a way, we had already begun to mourn... Not outwardly, of course, but in our hearts: lamenting the end of our supposed future relationship with Mum (grandma), for which we had all unintentionally prepared and graded our grief according to each ability and skill that she seemed to be losing.

For me, recognizing that this new partnership would be unique and a "journey together" was crucial.

Identifying the advantages

Life became about finding ways to support Mom in leading the greatest possible quality of life.

It was difficult, annoying, and depressing, but it was also happy, funny, cozy, loving, and fulfilling. Furthermore, I think that having Alzheimer's has provided me with more time to get to know my mother better, learn new things about her, go on new adventures with her, and grow to love her even more.

I can understand why there is so much negative stigma associated with dementia. It is a terrible illness that gradually kills the brain, erasing memories, cognition, understanding, emotions, speech, and physical capabilities. It's been called the slowest death, and for families, it can be the longest mourning experience.

However, now that my mother's second anniversary has passed, I wanted to share the blessings, the pleasure, the learning opportunities, and the triumphs that Mum's dementia has brought to me.

Lesson 1: Trips ought to be organized.

The latest advice is to plan ahead and be less ambitious, but don't shy away from trying new things. Always have a fallback strategy. Have a good sense of humor.

I used to take Mom on day outings while her dementia was still in its early stages. Taking the local transit allowed her to maintain her connection to the past.

She would become more nervous when she forgot how to produce her card for the scanner, which would often irritate bus drivers. However, one motorist was really amused when I insisted on showing him my own OAP pass (I was just 50 at the time). And on the way to town, she happily talked to a toddler, forgetting about her own discomfort.

Everything was going great on a day trip to Skipton until I started to aimlessly wander around the market (something she and Dad had always loved to do). She scowled and gave me the "black look" every time I steered toward a stall, but it all went away when I stated that there was a little tea shop with coffee and cake!

Mom was a huge fan of visiting coffee shops. Mum found the modest and unadorned ASDA cafe to be 'lovely' in her later years. However, my favorite excursion was to Harrogate's Betty's Tea Rooms. We had a brunch with silver service, courteous servers and waitresses, and trolley-borne pastries. Mom cherished it.

My main concern was how to "visit the ladies" with an elderly sweetheart who might disappear while I was still in my cubicle. Many thanks to all the strangers who 'watched' Mom for me on our day trips!

Lesson 2: People with dementia benefit greatly from singing.

 New knowledge: Singing makes you happy and releases endorphins. Never give thought to what others may think. Have a good sense of humor.

Anything with a beat, whether it's hymns, classic songs, musicals, or nursery rhymes, is fuel for the soul. Singing improves brain function. It helps us rekindle our feelings and memories.

To our surprise, Mum could still sing along to songs at the least hint, even as her short-term memory deteriorated and she lost her identity and her ability to speak. additionally in tune.

Our final excursion as a group was to watch South Pacific at Leeds' Grand Theatre. After taking a few minutes to settle into our circular seat, she expressed her desire to go. As the lights went down and our row got more and more crowded, I could feel the panic mounting. I didn't have to worry.

Her expression brightened the moment the orchestra started the first few measures. She performed each song. aloud.

I was ready with a canned response for when anyone in the vicinity voiced complaints, but none did. She was changed for those two hours, so I wouldn't have stopped her. Joyful, serene, and strangely connected.

She gripped my arm securely as we walked back down the luxurious staircase and into the daylight. "Why are we in this place?" With trepidation, she asked, "Are we heading home now?" And that instant passed.

We glanced over the program together on the bus, but she was unable to recall anything from the pictures. However, I will never forget the day she sang at the Grand!

Lesson 3: Memory can be improved by reading and reciting.

New insight: You should never assume that someone couldn't surprise and astonish you with what they can retain just because they appear to have lost their memory or word recall! Keep feeling amazed and in amazement all the time.

Mom was an ardent reader of illustrated children's books and never lost her passion for reading. Favorites included Raymond Briggs and Julia Donaldson.

All of Beatrix Potter's stories were read aloud to us and alongside us, including The Gruffalo, Room on the Broom, and The Giant Jam Sandwich, as though she were reading to her own children—which, of course, she was!

She would admire the colors and use her thin fingers to trace the lines, or she would laugh at the pictures and explain the scene on each page.

"That soars above valleys and hills," Mom retorted. She continued, reciting the full poem by Wordsworth with exquisite emphasis and tone.

I tried again: "There is nothing more fair that Earth can display."

She went on, "Dull would he be of soul who could pass

by?" in a lower voice. Taking it all in stride, she again repeated the poem word for word, displaying a devotion and emotion I imagine she was taught in school some 70 years ago. It would make Wordsworth proud.

That day is something I will always remember.

Lesson 4: Life skills are not merely acquired.

Newfound wisdom: Never presume that someone is incapable of performing domestic chores just because they are unable to accomplish them on their own.

Mom used to take great pride in cleaning, dusting, and vacuuming the house. Her day was shaped by these 'chores'.

There were moments when, as Alzheimer's spread, she would either follow us nervously or sit and look blankly.

One day, I gave her a duster, and she began to dust the bookshelves happily, not quite as precisely as before, but it kept her busy until she said, "What else are you going to make me do?" My moral bubble broke as a result!

Another day, I was baking—a skill that our mother had taught all three of her children—and our offspring were now carrying on the family legacy with our grandkids!

Mom stared at the flour and scales, obviously not comprehending when I asked if she wanted to help. However, she decanted the ingredients with care and then followed my example to mix and knead the dough. She was confused by the rolling pin and biscuit cutters at first, but once she had the dough in her hands, she rolled it skillfully and enjoyed cutting the shapes out. She was shocked and delighted to learn that she had made the biscuits when we later dipped them into a steaming cup of tea!

Many of us actually enjoy ironing. Yes, I believe I have inherited this from my mother! Mom, though, was exacting. She ironed everything to perfection, pressing the collar edges precisely and flattening the facings, but she was too risk-averse to continue doing this alone. She would burn herself or scorch clothes.

Rather, she would go through a stack of blouses or tea towels, and we would sit and talk. Here she was, her brain shrinking notwithstanding, concentrated, focused, doing something useful, doing anything.

I went to my mother's house with some fabric and templates to make bunting for my daughter's wedding. In preparation for my sewing, we had a great time cutting out, ironing, and matching up colorways. And while Mom was unable to come in person, it was a beautiful way for her to be there at the wedding.

Mum used to 'assist' when she was in a care facility later in life by folding the napkins or washing. I believe that caregivers frequently pass up chances to interact with their patients and to help them resume their everyday routines.

You may retrain yourself to perform simple tasks like folding towels, napkins, and arranging a table. This can help someone regain attention and overcome their seeming unresponsiveness. It combines diversion and activity in one.

Lesson 5: Play and exercise are essential.

Newfound knowledge: Never assume that a person with dementia who seems "frozen," uncommunicative, or distant would not be able to participate in play and physical activity. Never undervalue the importance of having fun!

As Mom's dementia got worse, I began reading more about the illness. I completed a Dementia Care certificate program and saw films featuring Teepa Snow, whose positive approach and "hand-under-hand technique" were incredibly helpful. Having watched 'Move it or lose it' with its creator, Julie Robinson, I was inspired by her regimen of sitting exercises.

Even though I was learning more about the illness, it didn't make the sense of powerlessness, annoyance, or sadness that caregivers experience from this incurable illness go away.

When I helped out one afternoon while my sister was at work, I saw that Mom's hand-eye coordination was still very good. I'd heard the same Julia Donaldson story far too many times, and it was too rainy to go for a stroll. It has been a long day already.

While I was on the phone with Mom, she got irritated

and began banging on a table in a quite truculent manner. I threw a small, soft teddy to her from where I was sitting, too far away to reach her. She threw it back and caught it with lightning speed! She was ready for my comeback throw, a cheeky gleam in her eye. Her attitude had changed.

After that, we would frequently play seated throw-and-catch games with bean bags, soft toys, and softballs. She was incredibly accurate and quick. Her mood swings and changes in demeanor used to intrigue me.

Playing catch would assist her to surface' in later years, even when she seemed empty and disengaged. And as she got more lively, we could tell that it was turning on certain areas of her brain.

If there were more players, Mom would enjoy the game

more and would choose who to throw to and whether to throw underarm or overarm. Occasionally, she would deliberately fling herself out of reach before joyfully pumping her fist—another novel and unusual motion!

I used shredded carrier bags and pipe-lagging to make cheerleader pom-poms. We utilized bubbles, balloons, and indoor frisbees, which worked less well.

While playing, we would occasionally recite nursery rhymes or the alphabet. We used to sing her a song occasionally. Not only did it provide Mom joy, but it also made us grin!
It was also a secure form of exercise. She would always find it amusing when we had to explain why she needed to take a break because she was enjoying it so much.

I believe that sometimes people are hesitant to conduct activities with older people that we typically identify with our youth, as if it would be interpreted as offensive in some manner. All of us, however, have a child inside of us, and the memories that fade first in dementia are the most recent ones—our adult selves. At last, we start to remember our early years more clearly. So why not make contact with those bygone days?

Lesson 6: Unwavering love

A new understanding: dementia does not require love, even when it takes away our skills and capacities.

Mom grew increasingly 'locked in' as her mental capacity diminished. Though I'm sure she knew we were the ones who trusted and loved her, she had forgotten who we were.

Mom would occasionally become agitated; these moments usually occurred when she was afraid or confused about what was going on or what we were asking of her. She quickly gathered a number of plush toys, which she would sit on and caress or touch.

We found that she could relax with the aid of a baby doll. She would rock the baby to sleep and tenderly caress it in her arms. She was a frequent walker, so when she received a pushchair for her doll, she had something to aspire to. Her tender touch never left her.

Lesson 7: Create more fresh experiences.

New insight: Make the most of this period by creating new memories, learning new things, and forging new bonds with your loved ones.

We made memory books with photos and our own recollections of Mom's activities as her memory deteriorated. These turned into topics of discussion for caregivers and us.

They made it easier for caregivers to get to know their mother before Alzheimer's.
Although I believe that not all of the care home workers read the bios we created, we made an effort to encourage them to do so. Later, Mom would read them and not be able to relate anything to herself; finally, she would stop reading, but the pictures were still interesting.

Even though they are priceless to us, the photo albums that would have captivated her during the early stages of dementia were uninteresting to her in later years.

Observing those intimate and joyful moments throughout my mother's protracted battle with Alzheimer's illness made the 200-mile round trip worthwhile for me.

I can relive those priceless moments with the help of pictures and videos. Therefore, even though I wish Mom hadn't had to go through this, I am incredibly grateful.

My mom and I were able to interact in ways that would not have been possible without dementia.

Chapter 11: Caregiver Resources and Tools

A person with dementia may experience a wide range of symptoms, including personality changes, memory loss, and strange behavior that is severe enough to impair daily functioning. Dementia is not a specific disease. Declaring someone to have dementia acknowledges these changes in the individual, but it does not explain the cause of these symptoms. It does not indicate the reason.

This section covers a wide range of topics, including understanding dementia, managing challenging behavior changes brought on by the disease, helping a person with dementia with everyday tasks like eating, cleaning, and taking care of themselves, as well as how to handle driving and managing caregiver frustration.

Good places to start looking for information:

A Guide for Caregivers to Understand the Symptoms of Dementia

An online learning series called A Caregiver's Guide to Managing Challenging Dementia Behavior

While providing care for a loved one suffering from dementia can be difficult, having the appropriate resources can really help. I employ specific techniques as a committed dementia caregiver to assist me in taking care of Mom.

Equipping yourself with useful and innovative tools can, in my opinion, improve the caliber of care you deliver. Continue reading for a list of the 8 tools that every caregiver for a dementia sufferer ought to have!

Apps for Medication Management

Medication monitoring is essential for dementia care. Using apps for medication management, such as Medisafe, to keep track of dosages, schedule medications, and create reminders. They can be helpful for a family member with dementia to share or for an individual with dementia to manage their medications alone.

Mats, fall and door sensors, and safety alarms

Dementia-affected loved ones may wander, endangering their security. To protect your loved one's safety and your peace of mind, install safety alarms, door sensors, and safety mats like Mat on Guard. These will notify you when doors are opened or if your loved one is moving around at unusual hours or getting out of bed late at night.

Zoned areas on certain security cameras can also detect when someone enters or exits a designated area. Additionally, personal sensors that can be worn as pendants and fall sensors are available.

Smart and Motion Sensor Lighting

Make sure the home has enough illumination; this is one of the best strategies to prevent falls. My mother requires high lighting to notice objects around her, as I have experienced. When mom was able to walk, we started using motion sensor night lights to light her room and the hallway leading to the bathroom. These were really helpful in reducing Mom's disorientation when she initially woke up and in directing her to the restroom.

Since then, we've added a sunrise clock to help mom wake up gradually and understand when it's time to get up. However, since we have caregivers, it may be very unsettling to be awakened early in the morning by strangers. To welcome her to the new day, I enter first thing every morning, precisely when the sunrise clock reaches its zenith.

Finally, we outfitted the house with smart lighting. The bedroom has a smart light. You can purchase several kinds of smart light bulbs or smart light systems, such as Philips Hue, to help light up your house and increase your loved one's safety!

Digital Reminder Systems, Clocks, and Calendars

Digital calendars, reminder systems, and talking clocks like the Robin Talking Clock with Day and Date can help your loved one stay organized.

Confusion and anxiety can be decreased by organizing appointments, everyday tasks, and significant events with the use of Google Calendar or apps like Remember The Milk. There are a ton of to-do list apps available, but why not stick with Google Tasks or Microsoft To-Do instead?

Apps for Cognitive Stimulation and Memory Aids

Improve cognitive performance with engaging apps and memory aids intended for dementia patients. Games and activities on apps like Lumosity and Mindmaze can support the maintenance of mental and cognitive function.

Alternatively, employ low-tech memory aids like checklists, huge visual calendar displays, notes in conspicuous places about the house, or a memory book with significant names, dates, and events that can help with remembering.

Apps for Communication

Using note boards, wipe boards, graphic dictionaries, or communication apps like TouchChat or LAMP Words for Life might be helpful when vocal communication becomes difficult. These apps offer several ways to communicate, which might help you stay in touch with your loved one.

But keep in mind that talking and comprehending what a loved one is saying can also be facilitated by taking your time and paying attention.

Adaptable and comfortable clothes

It can be difficult for someone suffering from dementia to dress. Wear comfortable, user-friendly, adapted gear to streamline the procedure. Putting on and taking off clothes can be easier if they include Velcro fastenings, elastic waistbands, and soft materials. You can create your own or try shops like AdaptaWear or The Able Label, among others. I sewed my mother a garment with velcro openings to fit in her emergency hospital bag, saving her from having to wear those hideous showing gowns.

Cameras and monitors

Put surveillance cameras in public spaces so you can watch your loved one from a distance. In order to be in touch with my mother while I'm upstairs doing chores and other things, I use an Amazon Echo Show during the day and a baby cam at night. This enables you to ensure their safety and well-being without being overbearing, particularly if you're a lone caretaker.

Consider privacy concerns and make sure usage is approved before installation.

11.1: Online Resources and Support Groups

Web-Based Materials

The Alzheimer's Association has a ton of research, articles, videos, and resources.

National Center for Aging This page provides useful information about caring for people with Alzheimer's and similar dementias.

Caregiver Action Network: This page offers information not only for caregivers in general but also for those who are providing care for a person with dementia.

Locate a Community: Using this tool, you can locate a

nearby senior living facility that offers memory care and respite care.

Support Teams

It's critical that you chat with people who are cognizant of your situation. Joining a support group is a beneficial way to talk about your feelings and experiences with other caregivers of dementia patients in a nonjudgmental setting. Here are some other resources for help, in addition to looking through your place of worship and local elder services organizations:

Alzheimer's Association: Look for a chapter in your area.

Facebook Support Groups: Two of the various groups to look into are as follows:

Dementia Support Group for Caregivers

Alzheimer's and Dementia Support for Caregivers

11.2: Recommended Reading and Additional References

Books

Creating Happy Memories Throughout the Alzheimer's Path: A Handbook for Families and Caregivers

Acquiring Knowledge on Alzheimer's: An Innovative Method for All Those Coping with the Illness

How to Deal with a Known Dementia Patient: Useful Tips for Families and Caregivers

The 36-Hour Day: A Handbook for Families Managing Individuals with Alzheimer's Disease, Associated Dementias, and Cognitive Impairment

Videos and articles

Managing Behaviors Associated with Dementia: Making the Switch to Memory Care

Ten Practical Methods for Providing Dementia Care

How to Encourage Alzheimer's Patients to Live Well Rather Than Just "Fade Away"

The video, "The Art of Living with Dementia," shows how one caregiver empowered, inspired, and improved the quality of life for individuals suffering from dementia and Alzheimer's disease by utilizing the arts, creativity, humor, education, and technology.

The video, "Art and Dementia," As dementia advances, it becomes more and more difficult to interact with loved ones who are suffering from the illness. Programs that link these people with art, however, offer unexpected exchanges and clarification.

Caregiver Tactics (video series): Learn how to maintain a relationship with your loved one by listening to what has helped others.

Products and Technology

The Best Apps for Caregivers

Technology-Based Solutions that Simplify the Care of the Elderly

Ten Vital Locating Aids for People with Dementia

Information from the Alzheimer's Association about technology in general.

AbleData: To find products that could be useful for daily care, search this database using the terms "dementia" or "alzheimer's."

You're not alone in your caregiving journey, no matter where you are in it. As you evaluate memory care options for your loved one, your family has access to tools and support.

The American Seniors Housing Association (ASHA), a well-respected advocate in the senior housing sector, powers Where You Live Matters. ASHA's main priorities are research, networking opportunities, legislative and regulatory advocacy, and education for senior living executives to help them better understand the needs of older people in the nation.

Dive deeper into the realms of health, self-help, parenting, and relationships with Michael J. Capps' collection of empowering books. Elevate your well-being and enrich your life through his insightful writings. Search for his transformative works using the barcode below

www.ingramcontent.com/pod-product-compliance
Lightning Source LLC
Chambersburg PA
CBHW051553250726
48653CB00004BA/1126